The Ferrari in
the Bedroom

*Also by Jean Shepherd
in Large Print:*

A Fistful of Fig Newtons

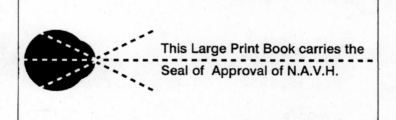

This Large Print Book carries the
Seal of Approval of N.A.V.H.

The Ferrari in the Bedroom

Jean Shepherd

With Drawings by
the Author

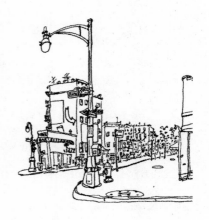

WHEELER
PUBLISHING

Copyright © 1970, 1971, 1972 by Jean Shepherd.

"The Ferrari in the Bedroom," "The Drive-In Confessional," and "Harold's Super Service" first appeared in *Car and Driver* and are reprinted here with permission of *Car and Driver*; "Great Expectations; or the War of the Worlds" first appeared in *National Lampoon* and is reprinted here with their permission; the song "Harold's Super Service," by Bobby Wayne, is quoted by kind permission of Shady Tree Music.

Published in 2006 by arrangement with Broadway Books, a division of Random House, Inc.

Wheeler Large Print Softcover.

The text of this Large Print edition is unabridged.
Other aspects of the book may vary from the original edition.

Set in 16 pt. Plantin by Minnie B. Raven.

Printed in the United States on permanent paper.

Library of Congress Cataloging-in-Publication Data

Shepherd, Jean.
    The Ferrari in the bedroom / by Jean Shepherd ; with drawings by the author.
        p. cm.
    ISBN 1-59722-180-5 (lg. print : sc : alk. paper)
    1. United States — Social life and customs — 20th century — Humor.   2. Humorous stories, American.
3. Large type books.   I. Title.
PS3569.H3964F4 2006
    813'.54—dc22   2005033693

To Frank and Julie Wald
who inspired a helluva lot of this

As the Founder/CEO of NAVH, the only national health agency solely devoted to those who, although not totally blind, have an eye disease which could lead to serious visual impairment, I am pleased to recognize Thorndike Press* as one of the leading publishers in the large print field.

Founded in 1954 in San Francisco to prepare large print textbooks for partially seeing children, NAVH became the pioneer and standard setting agency in the preparation of large type.

Today, those publishers who meet our standards carry the prestigious "Seal of Approval" indicating high quality large print. We are delighted that Thorndike Press is one of the publishers whose titles meet these standards. We are also pleased to recognize the significant contribution Thorndike Press is making in this important and growing field.

Lorraine H. Marchi, L.H.D.
Founder/CEO
NAVH

* Thorndike Press encompasses the following imprints: Thorndike, Wheeler, Walker and Large Print Press.

Introduction

For the past eight or nine years (I have no idea under what circumstances I began) I have accumulated around me an enormous, flowing collection of published Straws In The Wind. Almost from the beginning I fell into the habit of calling this ramshackle and growing mountain of crumpled, torn, dog-eared bits of paper my Vast File Of Dynamic Trivia. Somewhere behind it all I had a vague idea that one day, when I pass on to my just reward, I would leave this enormous heterogeneous mess to, say, the Smithsonian Institute, or maybe the Rotary Clubs of America, to be preserved for future generations so that one day they will know How It Really Was.

I have never been able to understand those poor unfortunates who turn to Literature, the Theater, the Cinema for universal truths or insights into contemporary life. How can this poor synthetic rubbish ever compare with even the mid-week edition of the average American newspaper, or a typical sampling of Junk Mail that arrives in our mailbox daily for a genuinely accurate reflection of the gullimawfry, the hilarious High Camp comedy that is Life itself?

H. L. Mencken, back in the Twenties, conducted a monthly column in his magazine *The American Mercury* that he called "Americana." It consisted of newspaper clippings, etc., gathered from the then 48 states of the Union. Re-reading these collections today is like suddenly, magically opening a window offering a clear vision of an earlier age. It is far more meaningful than any of the novels, the plays, the movies turned out during the same era. It is difficult to read two paragraphs of these columns without breaking out into genuine old-fashioned belly laughs.

It is my thesis that our time too should be preserved in like manner. Too many authors are spending too much time writing about their bruised psyches, their unending search for a beautiful Identity; the eternal undying, unselfish love of a Good Woman or whatever, and not enough bothering to even recognize that something is going on out there.

Commencing with this book, I propose to dip at random into my Vast File Of Trivia to pass them along to the reader for whatever value they might have. Most of them require no comment; others do. I am not intending, however, to limit my exhibits to the U.S., as Mencken did. We live in a time when it is almost universally thought among many highly respected savants that the American and the American way of life are the chief creator and the repository of Idiocy of all forms. This is questionable.

We begin with a little-reported incident that occurred at that great beehive of fantasy, dream, intrigue and connivery: the United Nations:

TAIPEI, FORMOSA, OCTOBER 12 (REUTERS) *Nationalist Chinese legislator Wong Kai-hau today demanded the recall of one of his country's delegates to the UN. The delegate reportedly fell asleep during an October 9th speech by an Algerian delegate recommending the admission of Communist China. Wong said Wen Yuan-ning was awakened by the applause of the Communist bloc and joined in the cheering.*

Somehow I feel a peculiar sympathy for Wen, as I have had similar occurrences at Sales meetings and other Inspirational gatherings.

Speaking of Inspiration, here is an Educational note received by one of our Spies:

As a graduate of International Correspondence Schools, you will receive Ambition four times a year. So that we may keep our mailing list up to date, please notify the editor of Ambition whenever you have a change of address.

Speaking of the wide world of opportunity, here is a recent advertisement clipped from that venerable grey old lady just off Times Square, *The New York Times*:

Wanted. Professional flagpole sitter. STATE PREVIOUS EXPERIENCE. *Box 438 Times.*

Speaking of ads, from the same journal, a Religious note for good Christians everywhere:

An exceptional LP. 2547 — Christmas With Ed Sullivan, *featuring Ed's own Christmas stories including reminiscences of his many Show Business friends; among others Jack Benny,*

Moss Hart and Cardinal Spellman. A perfect gift.

Which reminds me, speaking of Show-biz, of a frighteningly symbolic note from a recent TV Guide movie listing:

The Giant Gila Monster (TV debut)
  After Teenagers disappear from an isolated Midwestern town, a giant Gila Monster invades the local Record Hop.

And dammit, I missed it!

But there is no doubt that we are living in the age of the Monster, in more ways than one. Monster wars, monster Politicians, monster people, Showbiz monsters and just plain Monsters. Here is a flash from the esteemed *Paterson (N.J.) Morning Call*:

Mrs. Jane Arnoldi sued for divorce on grounds her husband thought more of Frankenstein and other monsters than he did of her. Mrs. Arnoldi said her husband Charles continuously read horror stories instead of talking to her, and kept dozens of models of monsters such as Frankenstein around

11

the house. The thing that finally drove her out of the house, she said, was her husband's insistence on describing surgical operations in detail at mealtime and becoming angry when she failed to enjoy them as much as he did.

They'll want to know about Charles in the twenty-fifth century.

Some things are eternal, though, and I'm sure in that far away future that a few of our Literary efforts will survive. For example, a Cultural bulletin as released by the Associated Press from Zrenjanin, Yugoslavia:

Radivoje Mominski won an important International prize in 1938 for writing the world's shortest book. The title was WHO RULES THE WORLD? The answer, in the book, is just one word — "Money." The book was printed in English, German, French, and Serbo-Croat, and recently in Urdu. All four previous editions are sold out. Mominski has decided to print a fifth edition, with the one word text unchanged.

The truth will always have a market.

Perhaps just as unchanging are the great, swelling tides of human passion. Tennessee Williams has never written anything as searingly revealing as this brief, enigmatic cable from Tokyo, via AP:

Arrested for breaking into the home of movie starlet Sayuri Yoshinaga and shooting a pursuing policeman, Kenji Watanabe said he only wanted to tattoo his name on the actress. "I'm a great admirer of Miss Yoshinaga. I've seen every movie she's made and I wanted to tattoo my name on her arm or leg," said the 26 year old factory worker. Police say Watanabe was caught carrying a home-made pistol and a tattoo set.

The Silver Screen has always attracted crawling hordes of autograph hunters, but damn few autograph *givers*.

But then, who can explain the inscrutable Oriental? For example:

YOKOHAMA (AP) *The Cosmic Brotherhood Association of Yokohama has declared June 24th Flying Saucer Sighting Day. Boys and girls out on dates on that evening are urged to watch for space ships and send out "A friendly telepathic invitation."*

A Zen flying saucer nut is almost as exotic a bird as a Hollywood TV Writer Karate Kook. Both are highly symbolic of our day. Here is a meaningful report of a devilish incident that occurred in Los Angeles (where else?):

FIGHT — *A TV writer who has been studying Karate for six years and has been awarded all the belts that certify him Expert last week had his first chance to try Karate in actual battle. While leaving the freeway in Los Angeles, another driver cut across his path twice. They exchanged insults and challenges, and both pulled up. The other man leaped from his car and rushed toward the Karate expert. Before the Karate expert could unsnap his seat belt and wreak his devastating fatal blows, the other man, who was considerably smaller, hit him, knocked out three teeth, and drove off.*

It isn't always easy to remember Pearl Harbor and to have the right diploma or the proper degrees. More often than not, quick footwork and a hit in the mouth will settle everything.

These are unsettled days and it's hard to know which side you're on, particularly among the New Wave of unbridled young, as nicely illustrated by this dispatch from N.A.N.A.

According to This Week In Tokyo, *the latest game sweeping Japan is "Demo." Youngsters particularly play this game. This is how it is played. Two sides are chosen. One side is the Police and the other side the Demonstrators. They push and shout, oftentimes becoming violent and causing severe injuries. One of the most popular slogans is: "We Oppose Homework." The children do not like to take the side of the Police, so they toss and the losers become the "Police."*

People are playing "Demo" everywhere:

ST. LOUIS, MO. (UPI) *Street Commissioner J. E. Gibbler of suburban Pagedale complained yesterday that just as he finished posting a NO LITTERING sign, a passing motorist "Threw a sack full of beer cans, coffee*

15

grounds and lettuce leaves at me, laughed loudly and drove away."

Well, at least somewhere, someplace people are still living the simple, honest, basic life. We wish to report at this time a tragic incident which recently occurred in a simple peasant village in Portugal.

BRANGANCI, PORTUGAL (UPI) *Jose Antonio, a 78 year old farmer was trampling grapes barefooted in a barrel yesterday to make wine. He was overcome by the fumes, fell into the juice and drowned.*

The hectic pace of modern life, the age of the emerging Machine, of rampant Automation, of mind-boggling space shots, of brain-numbing traffic jams, not only takes its toll of us, the hapless human beings who created the monster of Technology but also those simple innocents who have the bad luck to inhabit a planet also populated by Man. We are in the midst of a giant struggle that goes on day and night all over the world. One day the battle will be over, the machines will have won, and few will remember the early days when the victims were falling.

16

FORT WORTH, TEXAS (AP) *The telephone rang as Mrs. F. A. Farnum was vacuuming her canary's cage. She wheeled to pick up the phone and — whoosh — up the vacuum cleaner nozzle went Joey Boy with one desperate "cheep!" Mrs. Farnum jerked the bag open, grabbed out her canary and desperately shook off a little dust. Joey Boy was still unrecognizable, so she put him under the faucet. Then, to be sure the bird didn't catch cold, she put him under her electric hair dryer. "He hasn't been singing since then," Mrs. Farnum said, "he just sits hunched over and stares a lot. But he's eating well."*

Ah, how like us all, hunched over, sitting, staring. But eating well. Not much singing, but a lot of staring.

Jean Shepherd
New York
September, 1972

Contents

Large parts of the following are fiction; other parts based on fact. Still others are pure mythology. Some characters are real, others are figments of a harassed imagination. To the real, I apologize. To the others, the back of my hand.

Jean Shepherd

I

I Hear America Singing; or "Leaves of Grass" Revisited

The nuttiness is spreading in our land.

I get on this plane recently. An emergency trip — out to Chicago and back again. No time to make reservations, and it seems that when you're really in a hurry the only seat you can ever get is on the Champagne–Red Carpet Flight. The others are all booked up weeks ahead of time.

And so I find myself going through this great big chute. You don't walk into airplanes any more; they inject you into them. The airplane is mainlining people. You walk through this tube — the same air-conditioning and Muzak that is in the terminal — you never know you're on a plane. It's like a big tunnel that runs from the Time-Life Building straight to Chicago.

This really is the Jet Age. In order to Keep Your Finger on the Pulse of Life you've got to do it at 700 miles per hour, or slightly below the sonic barrier. Because, baby, that's where it's happening. That is where the story is being spelled out.

But one thing — at subsonic speeds you've got to really look at it hard in order to see it, because sometimes it's moving so fast it's just a blur. Trailing smoke.

You've got the picture. I am injected into this enormous silver monster, floating gently on a sea of barely audible Muzak, the sweet Karo Syrup of Existence. I am strapped into my seat. My safety belt is a delicate baby-blue shade, matching the cloud-blue and spun-silver interior décor of this about-to-hurtle projectile.

Muzak rises to a crescendo and we take off. Instantly we are high over this big chunk of land, and the world has become a blurred Kodachrome slide.

A man today never feels so alive as when he is hurtling from one point to another on the azimuth. My nerves are tingling. I'm ready to devour Life in great chunks. In the Champagne–Red Carpet–First Class– VIP–Very Expensive Section.

Silently the red velour is rolled out and baby-blue and silver *houris* are plying me with stuff to eat — which if my mother knew I was eating she would really know I have gone to hell. By God, caviar and Moët *brut* and diced lamb's-liver pâté at 8:17 a.m., over Altoona.

Suddenly, with no warning, from behind me I hear the sound. I have never heard anything like this ever in a jet plane. Or in a biplane for that matter. Or even a Fokker trimotor. I'm sitting there knocking down the caviar, slurping up the champagne, when from behind me I hear the sound, the unmistakable twang, the soul-searing biting buzz of a *guitar!*

A plaintive G-minor chord mingled with the sounds of ice cubes and plastic swizzle sticks . . .

Boing . . . boing . . . twaaannng . . .

And then, a heartbroken voice. It's the voice of America Singing:

500 Miles! ! ! !

It echoes through the pressurized cabin, bouncing from one curved baby-blue bulkhead to the next, and finally fading out somewhere near the "Occupied" sign at the far end of our sealed capsule:

500 Miles! ! ! !

For crying out loud! A Lonesome Traveler! On a jet flight for Chicago, Meat

Packer to the World, City of the Broad Shoulders, where the fog creeps in on little cat's feet. A Lonesome Traveler in the Champagne–Red Carpet–First Class–VIP– Very Expensive Section!

I turn around. And here's this angry, beat-looking kid sprawled out there in his foam rubber seat, his safety belt unhooked, a battered guitar case beside him. This angry kid, all tanned from Fire Island where the Crusade for Truth is swelling like a mighty organ chord that cannot be ignored. He's tanned, and wearing a pair of Levis carefully torn in all the right places. It cost his old man a lot of bucks for that pair of Levis — torn, faded, and worn as if they've been worn building the Union Pacific by hand, fighting the Terrible Depression of the Thirties, scrabbling out of the stony soil a hard crust of bread for a poor, honest man, just a-livin' in This Land, just a-tryin' to Love and a-tryin' to Understand and Live as a simple, pure Heart with his Fellows, his Brothers and Sisters all over This Land. A pure White Dove, a-sailin', a-sailin', a-sailin' . . .

The Times They Are a-Changin'

This guy's singing there and the tears are

26

just a-streamin' down between the champagne glasses and the olive picks. . . . There was hardly a dry eye in the house. I am surrounded by a horde of college students, all empathizing like mad with the plight of the Common Man Fighting Against the Forces of Evil, the forces of a rotten, decadent Society.

This kid is on his way to his junior year at the University of Iowa, all the way Champagne Flight, all the way it's been all of his life.

If I Had a Hammer

There he sat, honest tears a-coursin' down those hardened, tan cheeks of his, hardened by so many hard, terrible, awful, wrenchin' scrabblin' weeks at Bar Harbor.

WE SHALL OVERCOME

He's getting *real* bugged now.

WE SHALL NOT BE MOVED

The stewardess bends over to say, "More champagne, sir?"

"Yeah, fill it up . . ."

27

If I Had My Way

I'm sitting there and all of a sudden I realize that today's Lonesome Traveler travels *only* First Class. And more and more I realized that the plight of the Common Man is now in the hands of the Uncommon Man. With plenty of jack.

One of the wildest things about this whole new Suffering Traveler bit that is spreading throughout the campuses today is that the higher a guy is in *actual* social status, the more he empathizes with the real strugglers. More and more you'll find that the "folk" groups are the most clean-scrubbed, most obviously well-heeled people you'll ever see in your life. You just can't imagine Peter, Paul and Mary *ever* hungry. Or Joan Baez, either, for that matter.

There I sit with champagne glass in hand, trying to figure out just exactly why all this vaguely bugged me. It reminded me of something else that I couldn't quite remember. Sort of like trying to remember just how *Swan Lake* goes, or something.

The guitar hit a lovely A-minor chord as the feckless youth behind me plumbed even deeper into his social consciousness. The stewardess's baby-blue bottom undulated up the aisle, toward Chicago. And suddenly I knew. Marie Antoinette! And then I recalled something out of my almost completely forgotten European history courses.

Marie Antoinette — now it came back. Just before the French Revolution . . . I could even remember a few pedantic phrases from my European History II textbook:

"Just before the French Revolution there was a tremendous upsurge of interest in and empathy for the peasant on the part of the idle nobility. It reached the point where Marie Antoinette and her ladies-in-waiting, with selected noblemen and their pages, would spend weekends in the country, dressed as milkmaids and simple peasants of the field."

Aha!

"In the forests around Versailles the decadent French court built simple peasant cottages in which to live the 'rough' life and to sing the praises of the rough singular man living his hard, stony life, tilling from the soil of France the barest essentials of existence. They actually *did* empathize with him. There was a movement led by Rousseau, the Rousseau Naturalism Movement. . . ."

I toyed moodily with a morsel of Belgian

mint jelly as behind me the Simple Peasant of the Field once again raised his sorrowful voice:

This Land Is Your Land

My left hand made the chord changes instinctively as he sang out.

Another section of European history came floating back to me on the scent of delicate candied baby yams:

"It is difficult to imagine what the *real* peasants and laborers and milkmaids of France thought when they observed Marie Antoinette and the noblemen at play. Some French writers believe that the sight so enraged them that the course of Revolution was then truly set."

Nervously, I signaled for more wine. I thought, high over Ohio, of the folk music audiences and singers I had seen. There hadn't been many downtrodden and defeated people in those crowds. Could it be that the lower down a man really is on the social scale, the less he identifies with the Folk Freedom Fighters, until finally, in the actual slums themselves, you'll find *no* guys singing:

This Land Is Your Land

I looked down through 37,500 feet of cumulus mist. I wondered how many guys were looking up out of tenements at this whistlin' lonesome jet carrying all these guys in the Champagne Section, winging on their way toward Northwestern, Indiana University, U.C.L.A., the University of Michigan. First Class.

A big blonde across the aisle, with an O.S.U. sticker on her Pan-Am flight bag, had joined in. Another white dove a-sailin' and a-sailin'. I wondered if that chick knew what a tumbrel was. Hard to say. American people are not historically minded. She probably thinks that a tumbrel is a seven-letter word (46 Across) meaning "a small cart."

A tall, skinny, crewcut kid, tweed jacket, Daks slacks, with a "Power to the People" button in his lapel, bumped past me, trailing the scent of Brandy and Benedictine. He was heading for the john.

Ban the bomb. I guess that kid figures that history started in 1945. Everything before that was some kind of bad TV show starring Rip Torn as the company commander who chickened out.

I started in on the mousse. Not bad. Ladyfingers soaked in Virgin Islands rum. The big blonde grinned at me over her copy of *The Realist*. Yes, by God, I was surrounded by Realists.

Another phrase from Eur. His. II jiggled into form:

"One school of thought holds that what happened in France can happen in any society at a certain point in that society's existence, when life becomes so unreal, abstract, to so many people that they begin to long hungrily for the life that they *imagine* is 'Real,' usually the life of men who are tilling the soil or suffering social injustices at the hands of the imaginers themselves."

Hmmmm. Seven or eight pilgrims had joined in the singing, led by a thin, sharp-faced, dark-haired, high-cheekboned girl in a burlap skirt from Jax. A nice bottom. I wondered if she knew what a tumbrel was.

This crowd was as much at home in a jet plane as they were in a taxicab. Belting it out:

I'm a lonesome, lonesome traveler
along the hard, rocky road of life . . .

sitting in the back seat of a Yellow Cab, the meter ticking away.

I'm a lonesome, lonesome Yellow Cab
Rider a-travelin' on the old man's
Diners' Club card.

One thing I've noticed about jet flying is that once you're at cross-country altitude, you rarely feel the slightest bump of a transient air pocket or rough crosswind. At 600 miles per hour plus, you just hang there, suspended. And it is easy to lose all sense of time, space, and reality. The old DC-3s and 4s and even the 6s bumped and banged along, and you knew damn well that something was out there battering at that fuselage, trying to get in. I guess the place to have a fantasy, if you don't want Reality to come creeping in on gnarled vulture claws, is in a jet, just hanging there.

I felt vaguely drunk. Every junkie and pothead I've ever known, as well as drinkers of all variety, somehow always use the word "high." By God, we really *were* high! Half a snootful at 37,500 feet is *high,* baby! Just look out of the misty, ovoid window and there it is, big, fat, and luscious — that fat old earth. I knew one guy who said every time he smoked a joint or two he felt as though he were slowly vol-planing around, doing an easy Immelmann, looking down at everybody. He could see it *all*. Of course, the truth is he was five feet six and a very nervous cat. In real life he didn't look down at much, except maybe a gopher or two, and it all

34

scared him. Maybe that's part of the key, too. I don't know.

The hostess began serving brandies and liqueurs. Our little First Class section was now a tightly knit, jet-propelled hootenanny. Bagged to the gills and feeling the rich, heady hot blood of Social Protest coursing through our veins. Solidarity! Love! Ah, it was good to be alive. And not only alive, but a vibrant, sensitive, Aware person who knew where injustice and human misery were. And we knew what to do about it. *Sing* about it.

I could no longer fight back the urge to join in with my fellow men. Yes, we had been through hell together. Together we had seen it.

A thin, pale young man stood in the aisle. His crystal-clear boy soprano quivering with exultation, he led us on to further glories. True, he reminded me a little of Jane Fonda, who never was exactly my type. His little-boy bangs carelessly brushed down over his forehead, his clearly symbolic denim-blue workshirt open, nay, *ripped* open, à la fist-fightin' Millhand, he was the very image of a Master Sufferer Singer of our time. In the overheated air of our First Class cabin you could almost see his head starkly outlined in a grainy black and white photograph — towering above the rubble of an American street — a perfect Album Cover head. One of the New Breed — the New Breed of fiction artists edging out the old crowd who had used writing as a medium to create fictional characters in novels and plays and short stories, characters that were clearly recognized as make-believe.

The New Breed has gone one important step farther. They use their own lives as a medium for fiction and their own persons as fictional characters. The New Breed can imagine himself to be anything, and believe it — Cowhand, Lumberjack, Negro, Itinerant Fruit-Picker, Bullfighter — any romantic figure that fits his fancy. So, at 19 or 20, a man can have lived a full, rich, dangerous life and feel that he is a worn-out, misery-scarred pilgrim. And what's more, his followers believe him, because they work in the same medium.

Denim Shirt's china-blue eyes burned with the feverish light of the Creative Artist, believing himself to be a rough-hewn hunk who had traveled many roads, "rode freight trains for kicks and got beat up for laughs, cut grass for quarters and sang for dimes," and now he was singing out all the pain of all those old wounds, a spent, scarred Singer for Truth who had been there and known it all. At 22.

If I Had a Hammer

sang the pale, wispy lad.

Up near the forward bulkhead two shaggy-browed 45-year-old tractor salesmen with the obvious tribal markings of retired paratroopers raised their snouts from the champagne trough. The port-side ex-sergeant glared backward down the aisle.

"For God's sake, sonny, will you keep it down?" With which the old battler went back to his jug.

For a brief moment the plane became very aggressive. A classical — if you will excuse the expression — pregnant moment.

And then, bravely, as he had always done, Young Fonda sang on. . . .

I looked at the bulging back of Old Sarge, and I wondered how many roads *that* old son of a gun had walked down. From Bizerte to Remagen, up the Po Valley and back; 7,000 miles, from Kiska to Iwo. And still on the Goddamn road.

Beat up for laughs! The grizzled specimen next to Old Sarge had the chewed ears of a guy who had fist-fought his way through every Off Limits bar from Camp Kilmer to the Kit Kat Klub on the Potzdamer Platz, and all for laughs.

The dark chick glowered up the cabin at the back of Old Sarge's head. He and his buddy were boffing it up. She glanced meltingly at young Denim Shirt, her blue and white "Get Out of Vietnam" button gleaming like an angry shield above her tiny black-T-shirted bosom.

Her glance spoke volumes: "Those clods! What do they know of Suffering, of fighting for Good, for Ideals? What do they know of the hard, flinty back alleys of Life, of Injustice? Only Youth *understands* and knows. Do not be afraid. I, an angry Girl-Type Lonesome Traveler, will protect you."

The lissome lad, taking heart, began again with renewed spirit and passion.

She was right. What *did* Old Sarge know about true Suffering? His swarthy, grizzled neck bent defiantly forward, back to the trough, that neck which still bore a permanent mahogany stain of 10,000 suns, the Libyan Desert, Tinian, the Solomons, Burma Road, Corregidor . . .

Chewed Ear glanced over his hunched shoulder for a brief instant at the button-wearer, the leer that had impaled broadbeamed, ripe-bosomed females from

Dakar to Adelaide, a glance primeval and unmistakable. She flushed. She obviously was not used to heavy artillery.

Blowin' in the Wind

The black-T-shirted White Dove fluttered, confused, in the sand for a few wing beats and then scurried out of range.

The undergrad hootenanny swung into the chorus. Someone had produced a Kentucky mandolin, jangling high above the passionate Ovaltine voices. . . . The cabin was filled with the joyous sound. Old Sarge, after the last note died echoing in the soft light-blue carpeting, turned suddenly. "Hey kid, do any of you guys know 'Dirty Gertie from Bizerte'?"

He laughed obscenely, not realizing he was disrupting a Religious service. The congregation plunked, embarrassed.

"How 'bout 'Lili Marlene'?" Without any warning, Chewed Ear tuned up — *a cappella.*

I've been workin' on the railroad,
all the Goddamned day . . .

He sang in the cracked voice that had sung itself out over 9,000 miles of Canadian-Pacific track, laying every spike in the frozen tundra personally.

I've been workin' on the railroad,
just to pass the time away . . .

he bellowed.

Blue Jeans in the seat behind me, in a put-down stage whisper to O.S.U. Bag:

"For God sake, 'I've Been Working on the Railroad'! This old guy wouldn't know a Work Song if he heard it."

The apple-cheeked youth, his fingers calloused by countless hours of guitar-pick-clutching, slumped knowingly against the cushions of his seat.

Can't you hear those whistles blowin' . . .

The whiskey-cracked calliope, honed and sharpened against the cold winds blowing over countless flatbed coal cars and short-coupled reefers, ground to a stop.

FASTEN YOUR SEAT BELTS. NO SMOKING PLEASE. The soft yellow warning broke up the action.

"This is the Captain speaking. We are making our final approach to O'Hare Airport. We should be on the ground in three

40

minutes. The ground temperature in Chicago — fifty-seven degrees. There is a slight crosswind. I hope you've enjoyed your trip. We hope to see you soon. Please fasten your seat belts."

Our great silver arrow knifed down through the thick underlayer of cloud and smoke. Red-roofed houses and lines of crawling blue Fords rose up toward us. The great flaps creaked and clanked into position. The bird paused for a brief instant, and we touched the runway.

"This is your stewardess. It has been a pleasure to have you aboard. Please keep your seat belts fastened until we come to a full stop. We hope you have had a pleasant trip, and hope to see you again soon."

The jet stopped rolling, and outside my porthole I could see the Chicago end of the Great Tube being inserted into our bird. Behind me, the angry snap of a guitar case clasp. We moved up the aisle. From somewhere ahead, a piping adolescent voice:

"Hey Freddie, I'll see ya next weekend at the big hoot in Ann Arbor. Dylan's gonna make the scene. Maybe Baez!"

Old Sarge, hat jammed down over his ears, made one last verbal swipe at the stewardess who stood by the exit as we

41

filed out. She smiled blandly.

"I hope you enjoyed your trip, sir."

Our little band of Lonesome Travelers toiled up the chute toward the City of the Broad Shoulders, Meat Packer to the World. The party was over.

2

"Straight Shooters Always Win"
. . . Dick Tracy

We sat in the warm afterglow of the Christmas celebration. My friend Clarence, an incurable romantic, and I quietly sipped a final glass of port. The family had long since gone to bed, leaving in their wake a billowing cloud of torn tissue paper, mangled ribbon rosettes and crushed boxes. The tree cast a mellow glow of Christmas cheer over the mound of presents, opened and admired earlier by the gang.

It had been, at least for me, one of the better Christmases — giftwise, that is. My usual lot of booty runs heavily to drab socks, glaringly unusable ties and bedroom slippers that pinch the insteps. Lately I've begun to feel that Christmas is for the other people. But this year everything was changed. As Clarence refilled his glass from the sideboard, I covetously toyed with the film advance lever of my magnificent new Instamatic Reflex. The Christmas tree bulbs reflected on the glowing surface of the 1.9 Xenon lens, making a tiny, multi-jeweled crown in the polished glass. I thoughtfully peered through the viewfinder, focusing a sharp image on the ground glass of a Christmas tree ornament that resembled a drunken Donald Duck. The family had really hit the jackpot with me this year. They had gotten me the Christmas present to end all Christmas presents, as far as I was concerned. I felt expansive and complete. My cup, while not totally runneth over, at least was decently well-filled.

"That is the most beautiful camera I've ever seen," Clarence said, raising his glass in a slight toast to the Instamatic. I leaned back comfortably in my easy chair.

"Well," I answered, "yes, it is a magnificent camera, Clarence. Certainly that is true. But I must say it is not the most beautiful camera I have ever seen. The best, for my purposes perhaps, but not the most beautiful."

Clarence carefully lowered his glass to the coffee table and, sensing something in my voice, quietly asked:

"What do you mean?"

"Old chum," I continued, "I've known you a long time. In fact, we've known each other since childhood." I sipped my wine thoughtfully.

"Yeess . . ." Clarence replied, a question in his voice.

"Clarence, do you think I'm an evil person?"

"Why, no!" He laughed at the thought of it.

"You are wrong, Clarence. I once pulled a job that I've never forgotten, and, in fact, that has kept me awake many a night over the years. And I got away with it."

I lit a cigar; blew a large smoke ring toward a rotund stuffed panda.

"What's all this got to do with the camera?" Clarence persisted.

"Okay, my friend. You are about to hear a confession. I have never told anyone about this before, and I trust I have your fullest confidence."

Clarence leaned forward with great interest: "Yes, of course! Go on. I'll tell no one."

"When I was a kid back in Indiana, my only form of reading matter was the comic strips. Like millions of others who now call themselves Grown-ups the chief influences in my early life were Orphan Annie, Flash Gordon, Buck Rogers and Mutt 'n Jeff. It was the Depression, and a kid in the Depression — at least in a Northern Indiana mill town — was not knee deep in toys. Or

45

SCHRAFFT'S

much else, other than snow, maybe.

"Every night I would read, or at least look at the pictures of the comics, with religious intensity. Even today I can remember lines uttered by Dagwood or Mr. Dithers, his boss. My kid brother and I would battle fiercely over who would get what page of the Sunday Color Comics, the absolute high point of the week.

"There were all kinds of great comics. Dick Tracy represented law and order and violence before the days of Gunsmoke. Polly and Her Pals was situation comedy à la Danny Thomas, while Smoky Stover was pure psychedelia. The whole spectrum of today's TV programming ran through the comic strips, including Mary Worth, in the Peyton Place tradition. There were even commercials, usually disguised as a comic strip running across the bottom of every Color Supplement sheet. Powerhouse Candy Bars had its own Superman, called The Powerhouse Kid. Peter Pain, a little, green, warty pickle with a derby hat, stuck pitchforks into ladies' backs on behalf of Ben-Gay salve. My kid brother and I, just like today's kids, enjoyed the commercials as much as the actual shows. Until one fateful Sunday when just such a comic strip commercial set me on the road to Crime."

Clarence, his eyes glowing with interest, hissed: "Yes! I remember those. Go on! What happened?"

"One Sunday," I continued, "occupying the half-page directly below Popeye and the Thimble Theater, was an enormous picture of a kid holding a magnificent Brownie camera. Gold colored, with a large seal embossed on the side. He grinned out of the page at me. Out of his mouth a white balloon carried this message:

KIDS! ANY OF YOU WHO WILL BE TWELVE THIS YEAR ARE GETTING A BIG PRESENT FROM THE EASTMAN KODAK COMPANY. IT'S THEIR BIRTH-DAY, AND THEY WANT TO GIVE YOU A CAMERA! FREE! GET YOUR DAD OR SOME GROWN-UP TO FILL IN THE COUPON BELOW, AND YOU'LL GET THIS SWELL CAMERA ABSOLUTELY FREE FOR EASTMAN'S BIRTHDAY.

Great Scott! I couldn't believe my eyes! A camera was something owned strictly by grown-ups and used only at major family celebrations, such as picnics and Grandfathers' birthdays. A camera! For kids! free!

The coupon read: I AM TWELVE YEARS

OLD THIS YEAR AND WOULD LIKE A FREE CAMERA ON EASTMAN'S BIRTH- DAY. There were blanks for name and ad- dress, and for an adult to sign, and then it said: TAKE THIS COUPON TO YOUR EASTMAN DEALER AND GET YOUR FREE CAMERA. YOU MUST BE ACCOMPANIED BY AN ADULT.

What a fantastic bombshell! There was only one trouble. I had just turned seven. For the first time my famous reading ability, which was the wonder of my family, had produced a traumatic experience.

Instinctively I knew what to do. I hid the coupon under the overshoes and fielders mitts in my closet and began to lay my plans. With the craftiness of a born crim- inal I created a foolproof caper. I knew my mother and father, being basically square and upright, would not sign any coupon saying that I was twelve.

The next day on the way home from school, I carried out the first step of my scheme. There was a candy store that kept me supplied with jawbreakers and rootbeer barrels which I had frequented for some time. I stopped by with three cents in the pocket of my corduroy knickers. This was roughly two-thirds of my Life Savings. I must confess that I am not much ahead of that level yet, but that's another story.

There was a tall, thin high school kid who worked at the candy store. He came from the neighborhood and was known to us all as Lefty Neff. He played first base on the high school ball team and was a local hero.

"Whadda ya want?" he asked as I peered into the glass case at a collection of juju babies.

"Two a' them."

"Okay." He handed them over and scooped up my penny.

"Hey, Lefty, have you got a camera?"

"What?" He was not used to this sort of question from the rabble of kids he dealt with.

"Have you got a camera?"

"Nah."

"Wouldja like to have one? To use, that is?"

"What are you driving at, kid?" I showed him the coupon.

"So what?" he asked.

"Well, I'm a kid," I said, "and you're a grown-up, and a grown-up, it says, can sign it for me."

Anyone over the Fourth Grade was a grown-up to me. Teachers were even beyond that. Thoughtfully he re-read the coupon.

"Yeahhh . . ." he said reflectively, "it might work." A crowd of kids came in at that point, so negotiations were broken off.

Two days later, after a bus ride of some length, the two of us walked into the big Eastman camera shop downtown. The window was crammed with golden cameras with big signs about Eastman's birthday party. The store was busy, as usual. I had only been past it from time to time and had looked in the window with my father or mother but had never been inside. It was an exciting place. Camera stores still make my old blood pound.

Lefty walked right up to a clerk who was wrapping something for a customer. He pushed the coupon across the counter. The clerk quickly read it, glanced up, and said incredulously:

"You his father?"

"Nah. I'm his uncle."

"Why doesn't he come in with his mother or father?"

"They was killed in a train wreck."

"Really?" The clerk peered down at me as I tried to look pathetic.

"Yeah. He's an orphan."

"He doesn't look twelve to me," the clerk observed, focusing his eyes sharply through his bifocals.

"He's little for his age."

"He sure is," said the clerk.

"They were in the circus," said Lefty in an attempt to change the subject.

"Who?" asked the clerk.

"His mother and father." He nudged me with his knee. It was my cue to talk.

". . . yeah!" I squeaked, "they were killed in a train wreck. I'm an orphan."

The kindly clerk's eyes watered. His bifocals clouded with sympathy.

"Yeah," said Lefty sadly, "when they got killed, he got stunted. From the shock."

"Oh, that's too bad," the clerk sympathized, "I'll call Mister Smythe. He has to okay it."

Uh-oh! Trouble! We waited a few minutes, panic rising, until Mr. Smythe, a tall, thin, balding man in a black suit, appeared. Apparently the clerk had told him the story. Mr. Smythe looked down at me and asked:

"Are you sure you're twelve?"

I was so scared that I couldn't answer. To this day I don't know whether Mr. Smythe was taken in or not. I'll never know. Maybe he was one of Nature's noblemen. Anyway, he said:

"Sonny, can you read that sign?" He pointed to a poster extolling the virtues of Eastman roll film. I read the first line. He stopped me with: "Charles, give the boy a camera. Mr. Neff, you have a precocious nephew."

"Yeah." Lefty used his favorite word.

Five minutes later we were on the bus home, with a brand-new leatherette-covered, gold-colored genuine Eastman Brownie, Anniversary model, with a roll of free film.

"Well, kid, ya got a camera," Lefty said to me as we got off the bus. "Now don't forget, I get to use it whenever I want, right?"

After I got home I carefully hid the camera in the coal bin and two days later announced that I had, astoundingly, found a camera, fully loaded, while on the way home from school. The family was rocked! It was a windfall of stupendous proportions. I was questioned sharply as to where and how the find was made. I carried it off flawlessly, now a hardened prevaricator.

I spent hours peering through the viewfinder, stroking the leatherette hide of my beautiful camera, clicking its shutter and pretending to take pictures long after the reel of film had been shot, by my father of course, at the Company Picnic. No camera I shall ever own will ever be as beautiful as that camera. Somewhere along the years it disappeared, but I've never forgotten it.

We sat, Clarence and I, for a long moment after I had finished the story. The Christmas tree glowed cheerily on into the night.

"Yes, I see what you mean. That must have been a beautiful camera," said Clarence softly, still in the mood of my tale of Evil.

"You know, Clarence, there are times when I fear every knock at the door, that one day an official of the Eastman Company will present himself, with an officer of the law. But I don't regret it. I would do it again."

Clarence drained his glass in a salute. "Well said."

I nodded.

Long after Clarence had driven out into the night I sat and toyed with my new Instamatic, planning future compositions; greater shots than before, then went up to bed. It was a good Christmas.

3

An Independent Survey
Today Announced . . .

News item:

TOKYO (UPI) *Honda Motors announced today that they are experimenting with a device to deal with the problem of drunken driving. It consists of a specially-treated platinum alloy disc which when fitted in the center of the steering wheel, detects the presence of alcohol on the breath of the driver, causing a relay to be actuated which prevents the car from starting. A prototype is under construction and will be tested shortly. Honda did not say what would happen if someone else in the car, say a mother-in-law in the back seat, had been drinking. They did say that results of their test would be announced as soon as available.*

Well, I guess it had to come. In this age

of Total Nervousness the car that comments on the personal habits of its driver was obviously a logical development. Not that I'm in any way, shape or form an advocate of drunken driving. On the contrary, I agree with any judge who really nails a guy who's been lappin' up the soup and kicking around 400 mean horsepower in addition. It's just that being told by your hardtop GT that you've made a horse's ass of yourself tonight smacks of further evils to come. Why stop with drunken driving? I say. How far can this thing go?

Well, anyone who has really done a hell of a lot of cross-country driving knows damn well that drinking is only one source of big trouble when it comes to the Clobbering scene. For example, how about battling with the wife? I would like to know the statistics on that one alone, just how many guys have powdered a safety island right in the middle of making the final crushing point in a screaming argument with the old lady over why the hell he acted like he did at his sister-in-law's house last night. With neck bulging, eyeballs popping, he screams, "God dammit, I never could stand that stupid broad even though she is your sis—" BOOMMM!

Okay, Nader, how you gonna handle that

one? After the Martini Meter has been installed universally and the accident rate continues to go up, no doubt someone, after an immensely expensive national survey, will come to the conclusion which we smart asses already know — that there are a hell of a lot of ways to prang a Buick that don't involve drinking at all. I can see a headline a few years from now:

ZAGREB (REUTERS) *The Zotz Motorwerken announced today that a new device to detect excessive battling in the car will be tested. The Uproar Meter, as it has been termed, is now in prototype and the results will be announced shortly. It consists of a sound-sensitive diaphragm which, when subjected to excessive yelling, cuts out the ignition, thereby immobilizing the machine.*

Naturally, after the installation of both the Martini Meter and the Uproar Meter accidents will continue to climb and statistics will soar. Nader will be nonplused momentarily but investigations into the causes will continue at spiraling expense. It will then be discovered that large numbers of accidents occur due to guys dozing off behind the wheel. This phenomenon does not necessarily result from a simple lack of sleep. For example, it is a well-known fact that large numbers of people find themselves totally unable to remain conscious in a Plane Geometry class in spite of twenty-two hour's sleep the night before. Others snooze off almost immediately when subjected to a David Susskind panel discussion. It is a well-known fact that many brains today are permanently in a state of vegetation bordering on catatonic sleep due to a prolonged overdose of unbroken, steady Hard Rock. For example, a driver is hunched over the wheel of his LDX 1750 Zotsmobile, as sober as a judge. In fact, he has refrained from drinking for forty-eight hours before taking the wheel, fully conscious that his car is watching him at all times. He is driving alone since he knows that taking a passenger with him may activate his Uproar Meter. He nervously hunches over the wheel, conscious that at any moment the Zotz may pull the plug on him. Boredom sneaks in. He flips on the radio.

". . . and I say to you, Senator Dubbleman, that the people of this country are now embarking on a sensitivity-awakening phase which will ultimately result in . . ."

"Just a moment, Susskind. Or can I call you Dave? Just the other day I was talking to Bella Abzug about that very thing, and as Arthur Schlesinger put it —" *Booooommm!*

INVESTIGATING COMMISSION DIS-COVERS BOREDOM CAUSE OF MANY ACCIDENTS.

We are now off again. Nader's Raiders embark on an Anti-Boredom crusade as accidents spiral once again. Since it is well known that Industry responds to the demands of the public, inevitably the following news item will appear:

AMANABAD, INDIA (AP) *The Maharaja Motor Corporation Ltd. today announced the development of a Boredom Detector. Since boredom is a major cause of auto accidents it is hoped that their new device will prevent this from occurring in the future. It consists of a highly-sensitive microphone which instantly detects the slightest snoring and measures the drop in respiration rate by the use of two electrodes embedded in the seat back. Tests are now being conducted on the Ennui Unit which, if successful, will be mandatory in all cars of the future.*

By the following year drivers of new cars, surrounded by Martini Meters, Boredom Detectors, Uproar Meters, safety belts (which by then will automatically overpower and clamp the driver into his seat whether he likes it or not, grabbing him in an octopus-like grip actuated by Selsen motors) will continue to smash themselves into oblivion with reckless abandon. New committees will be formed, especially those calling themselves *ad hoc*. Crash programs will proliferate and once again Nader's crowd will ride full cry into the fray. Within two weeks of the delivery of the first new models so equipped, the following will occur:

HE: "You sure you haven't been drinking, baby?"

SHE: "Not a drop for two weeks."

HE: "Me either. Now keep your voice low. We don't want no hassle. This baby is sensitive."

SHE: "Don't worry. I feel nothing but kind thoughts for the world."

HE: "If you start feeling bored, fer

Chrissake lemme know."

SHE: "Don't worry, I'm on my toes, alert."

HE: "Good."

(They hum along nicely for several minutes.)

HE: "Hey baby, you know there's something about the way them streetlights light up your profile that just . . . well . . . *Boy!*"

SHE: "You're cute too, Harold."

HE: "Your skin is like vanilla yoghurt, your eyes like . . . just one little kiss!"

SHE: "Oh Harold!"

HE: "Oh Marsha!"

SHE: "OH Har—"

Booommm!

SEX DETERMINED MAJOR CAUSE OF AUTO CRASHES. WASHINGTON (UPI) *The Ad Hoc Concerned Committee of Involved Citizens For Auto Safety reported today to public safety czar Ralph Nader that their 26-month high-intensity field investigation of auto accidents has come to the conclusion that 43.9% of crashes today are caused by, as the committee put it, "amorous misadventures." Nader promised immediate action.*

SPITSBERGEN (AP) *Norgemot, the Scandinavian Motor Combine, released today a report on its new Sex-O-Stat which is now being road tested. Consisting of a built-in blood pressure measuring device and an associated thermostatic heat detector which reacts to the sudden increase in body heat due to sexual excitement, the combined unit is known as a Sex-O-Stat. When blood pressure and body temperature rise to a dangerous point the Sex-O-Stat shuts down the engine, rendering it harmless. If successful, it will be mandatory on all future cars.*

Stone sober, icy calm, alert and gelded, within a month of the delivery of their new Norgemot XD/712 Zuds, two drivers, Anton Klautski, 67, of Glendale, California and A. J. (Bucky) Whippersnade, 19, of West Peapack, New Jersey, will have both mysteriously splattered themselves and their Zuds over their respective turnpikes.

AUTO ACCIDENTS CONTINUE TO MOUNT NATIONWIDE. PRESIDENT NADER EXPRESSES CONCERN.

Once again conferences blossom and in-depth surveys accelerate to determine the mysterious causes. Thirteen months pass as an anxious world awaits.

AGE CRUCIAL FACTOR IN ACCI-DENT RISE, COMMISSION FINDS. World-wide statistics prove conclu-sively that an overwhelming number of accidents of a fatal nature are caused by drivers under the age of 31 and over the age of 44. Accident rates for those under 30 statistically soar, says the report, and are matched only by those drivers over 44. The conclu-sion is obvious, the report went on. President Nader expressed his deep concern and promised immediate leg-islation.

NAIROBI, KENYA (UPI) *Kenya Kars, Inc., today startled the auto world with its new Chron-O-Stop, a revolutionary device which instantly detects the chronological age of the would-be driver. Consisting of a microscopic needle embedded in the ignition key, it takes a minute blood sample of the driver. Through a computerized ana-lyzer it measures the calcium deposit in the bone joints of the subject,*

*placing the age accurately. It is be-
lieved that this device will supersede
the new Radium 14 age detection
system that was announced by
Formosa Motors last month. The Radium 14 method, while accurate,
tended to cause leukemia in its users.
The new device will be mandatory in
all upcoming models.*

In spite of the continuing proliferation of
safety devices, insurance rates will rise and
people will die like flies on the highways,
causing consternation on every side. Three
days after his new Kenyan Crocoblast
hardtop was delivered, 36-year-old, clear-
eyed, abstaining, non-amatory, completely
calm Marty Buglebaum was tooling along
US 66 at the ready. He turned to his friend
Max and said the following:

MARTY: "You know, Max, it is a fact
that Republicans represent the Establishment and big business, and I,
for one —"
MAX: "Now hold on, Marty. You
bleeding hearts that call yourselves
Democrats ain't got no sense of realism."
MARTY: "Realism, boy what a joke!

You guys just last year alone —"
Powwww!

*POLITICS LARGE ROLE IN ACCI-
DENTS. National statistics bear out
suspicions voiced recently by President Nader that registered Democrats
are involved in a far more significant
number of accidents than Republicans. In fact, 74.4% of fatalities in the
last calendar year were participated in
by Democrats, the National Under-
writers' publication* WHY? *charged
yesterday. Senator G. L. Fignewton
(Rep., Montana) demanded immediate Congressional action. President
Nader promised his unqualified sup-
port.*

Naturally, industry would immediately
swing into action and within a short time
would produce its infallible Pol-O-Graph,
based on the hitherto undiscovered fact
that Democrats are of a specific physical
type and perspire more copiously than Republicans, although less than Communists.
The instrument, based on rate of perspira-
tion, infallibly prevents those of dubious
political affiliation from operating any machine on any of the world's highways. The

safety-conscious everywhere breathed a sigh of relief that at last all problems have been solved.

Within weeks after the first politically safe, age-proof, bourbonless, sexless, non-agitated machine appears on the nation's highways, the inevitable would occur. Just outside of Erie, Pennsylvania, under good conditions, 32-year-old Agatha Schoonmutter, a schoolteacher, a non-drinking virgin Quaker pacifist, member of no known political party, while driving with her friend Helena Camembert was involved in the following:

AGATHA: "You know, Helena . . ." (glancing carefully at the speedometer to make sure everything is all right) ". . . I think we ought to consider bridge mix for the next card party at my place."

HELENA: "Why? What's wrong with the chocolate-covered cherries we've been having? And anyway, everybody likes them."

AGATHA: "That's true. Did you notice how fat Clarice is getting? And she's so catty! Sometimes I can't stand the way she shows off about that so-called man of hers."

HELENA: "Oh, *him!* What I couldn't tell her about him, if I wanted to!"

AGATHA: *"Really?* Come on, how about the dirt. I won't breathe it to a soul."

HELENA: (lowering her voice to a whisper) "Well, just listen to this. The other night, who do you think I saw coming out of the Pig And Whistle? With this busty, blowsy-looking blonde!"

AGATHA: (drinking in every word) "Really! Right here in town? Well, I can hardly wait to tell —" *Ka-powie!*

NATIONAL SCANDAL! FATAL ACCI-DENTS HIGHEST IN HISTORY.

Again graphs, charts, door-to-door inquiries, actuarial tables, the whole works go into full swing.

WOMEN LEAD MEN 2–1 IN FATAL ACCIDENTS. Statistics proved a startling fact yesterday before the Senate Investigating Committee headed by Representative Harold J. Upshaw of Rhode Island. "We have to face the fact at last that women far outnumber men in fatal crashes," he stated be-

fore television reporters today. President Nader, when informed, issued an immediate Presidential decree banning women from the road.

Again the battered nation sighs with relief, believing fully that at last the accidents that have plagued drivers since the days of Barney Oldfield have been all but eliminated. Alas, within eight hours of the new legislation thirty-six more catastrophic accidents occurred in scattered parts of the nation. By the following week it was realized that accidents were still on the rise. After seven weeks of deliberation at the Princeton Institute Of Higher Thinking, a top-level conclave of scientists, writers, artists, engineers, doctors, and the coaches of the two leading professional football teams in the NFL issued the following bulletin:

After reviewing all available material and only after consulting with all known experts from around the world, we have determined that in every case of fatal crash a person was involved. President Nader today made his position clear. He banned all human beings from automobiles under penalty of life imprisonment.

Within weeks, Zenith Motors of Belgrade Yugoslavia immediately announced its new driverless auto, which excludes humans of all sorts. The results are not yet in on this new experiment.

4

The Man of the Future
May Be a Woman

I wonder what the late A. J. Liebling would have thought of the current crop of hard-bitten, Hemingwayesque, tough-talking (and I presume Tobacco-chewing) females who are today covering boxing, baseball and dragstrip racing with all the verve and gusto of a Levi-wearing, baseball-capped girls' finishing school sophomore who has just found out that she loves to say *fuck* out loud with the rest of the boys.

This inanity came full circle when *Life* assigned someone named "Shana" to cover the Clay-Liston fiasco. *The Village Voice* has at least five people named "Barbara" who rhapsodize over Minor League ball-players with the same easy familiarity of a grizzled sportswriter who has spent thirty years in the sweaty, steamy locker room of the Moline club, the Three I League.

Just exactly how these two fantasies arose is difficult to ascertain at this point in time, since I believe we are just on the beginning of the upcurve, and God knows where it will end. Perhaps with Barbara herself taking on Shana for the Middleweight Championship of the World, and Tom Wolfe Indian-wrestling Andy Warhol for the number three spot on the Ten Best Dressed Women Of The Year list.

This surrender of masculinity by the male of the species and its resultant adoption of virility by the female has been gradually observed in the popular arts for some time. However, its growth is logarithmic, rather than straight line, which is to say the beginnings were gradual but now the curve is arching upward rapidly toward a final great explosion of Swap Identities. The word *identity* has been for at least fifteen years a favorite totem in Literary circles. If there has been one novel described as "A young man's search for his identity in 20th Century America" there have been ten thousand. They have all had, practically without exception, the same theme, saying more unconsciously than they knew. The word *identity* referred really to "what sex am I?" and the search for an answer was almost strictly a Male search. I can't recall many novels: "A young girl's search for identity in mid-20th Century, etc." offhand, and I doubt whether many were

73

written, primarily because the female *knew* where she was going. She was heading for the corner saloon, the Men's Shop in Macy's, and, if possible, the Third Base slot on the Dodgers. And it looks like she'll make it.

The male, however, was confused, since he had been conditioned from infancy to the ideas of an earlier age; the romanticism of a world in which men pursued women and women capitulated, and there was a thing called Love. It has been observed that the two sexes do not necessarily travel at the same rate of speed through time, and that the female of the species is perhaps more advanced into the 20th Century than the male. Hence the male's confusion as to what and where he is. The male is also, historically, not as adaptable as the female to changing conditions of life, so hence the transition into a new, impersonal, urbanized existence has not been as easily consummated by the man as it was by the woman.

The fascinating results can be seen everywhere. The romantic development of the male Beatnik of the early Fifties who tried to fantasize himself out of his time and developed great glass bubbles of fiction around his life, fervently imagining himself to be a 19th century cowhand, a fistfighting hobo of the Thirties, a Whaling sea captain, a Spanish bull-fighter, and God knows what else. The remnants of this fantasizing are still with us in the Bob Dylans, who once was quoted on a record jacket extolling one of his discs as having "Fistfought his way across America, singing for nickels and dimes." Poor little one-hundred-and-thirty-five pound Bobbie. I can't imagine who he fistfought with, but I'm sure he fervently believes he did. He is really the end product of the Kerouac era, with one difference but it is a significant one, and that is whereas Kerouac avowedly wrote Fiction, Dylan believes his, and would bridle at the idea that it was pure fantasy.

Why do men in the 1970s find it necessary to dream themselves into another existence? Well, that's not so easy to answer, but I suspect it could be that the outside world, the world of Mao Tse-tung and the great void beyond, have become a little difficult to deal with. Children have always played House with interchangeable roles, and I suspect that great portions of our population are reverting to childhood in their moment of terror.

And of course there is that matter of Responsibility. This is one of those words that is slowly beginning to creep out of the language as others have in the past, like Honesty, Patriotism, Courage, and Immoral. It is fascinating to watch how closely language itself reflects changing times. H. L. Mencken was a dedicated student of this phenomenon, which led to the development of Semantics as a branch of The Humanities. *Responsibility* is a word that now is used almost exclusively to describe something that *Society* should have toward the individual and is hardly ever mentioned, if at all, in the reverse. In short, as we become more and more child-like and create a firmer foundation of fantasy for our lives, playing House with a vengeance, it is obvious that we must eventually reverse roles if we are to avoid personal responsibility. A male who has adopted a female role cannot be expected to have the responsibilities of Fatherhood, being feminine, and conversely a female who has clothed herself in the outward guise of masculinity should not be asked to wash the dishes.

And ultimately, of course, Sex will have to go too, since it obviously entails many dangers, such as who is going to do what to whom. And even more to the point, *why?* So the development of a race of Neuters sliding back and forth on the identity scale at will was inevitable; asexual, non-involved, self-loving, and almost entirely devoid of the more human compassions, and cruel to the extreme.

Cruelty is one of the most obvious characteristics of the output of the New Neuter, both female and male, a kind of constant running Put-down of all the Others, the Others, of course, being those who are, for one reason or another, Out.

The ascendancy of the Girl as top dog, or shall I say top bitch, in our society has created some exotic byproducts. Among them is the male Soap Opera. A Soap Opera can be defined as a sexual fantasy wherein the chief character is triumphant in all situations and maintains an air of superiority through great perils and incredible catastrophes, but always remains successful in the end. Helen Trent was the great prototype of the Soap Opera world. Even her tag-line was highly significant: "The program that answers the age-old question — Can a woman of thirty-five attain true Love?"

You bet. At least old Helen did. Every male who appeared on the horizon immediately went ape, threatened suicide, suffered amnesia, developed catatonic blindness, and took to drink, all over the love of Helen Trent, which of course she withheld.

Helen Trent is so close to James Bond as to make one wonder whether the late Ian Fleming might have been an old Helen Trent fan. A few decades back, countless downtrodden women lorded over by an all-powerful male out having, at least so his woman thought, endless Fun At The Office mooned dreamily over the ironing board as Helen Trent, Wendy Warren, Mary Noble and other spectacularly sudsy ladies squelched, ground under heel, obliterated, loved and left male after male as the afternoon wore on toward that disastrous moment when Attila the Hun slammed the door open and hollered "Where's supper!" For her, Helen represented real life that was being lived somewhere Out There, and oddly enough was a spookily accurate harbinger of Career Girls to come. Countless offices today are riddled with steel-jawed, skiing, surfing, motorcycle riding Helen Trents that have about as much use for males as James Bond has for chicks.

Ah yes, James Bond. The new Helen Trent for a multitude of sunken-chested, bespectacled, Pepsi-drinking *Playboy*-reading, fantasy-ridden, lonely males. 007, the nuclear bomb of Passion (or at least Sex, and there is a difference, gentlemen) has become the will-o-the-wisp dream phantom of the great horde of those who prefer to read, or are afraid to date. The amazing number of males who today moon about Sex, read about it, see it in films, write about it and do everything but *have* it is highly reminiscent of the virginal ladies who in the 1930s and early 40s read *True Confessions*, *True Romances*, and gaped at Bette Davis epics of celluloid sensuality. The old novel of the beautiful sensual female has all but disappeared. Kathleen Winsor and *Forever Amber* are fragile period-pieces of another age, written for women who dreamed, to be replaced by the current crop of novelistic Male sexual fantasies of the Norman Mailer/J. P. Donleavy/Ginger Man stripe. Sebastian Dangerfield is the reading man's Amber. Fantasy studs who thunder their way through billowy fields of acquiescent females, untouched by any of them, triumphant to the end, but all with a wicked glint of delightful, boyish humor in their dancing eyes.

Exactly the way Amber St. Clair was described by an earlier fantasy merchant of an earlier era. Even the names are similar; Amber St. Clair — Sebastian Dangerfield. My god, will Sexual wonders never cease?

The women who read and quivered to Amber had as little real Sex in their lives as the nervous, hollow-cheeked, gaunt admirers of Philip Roth have in theirs. And for the same reasons. They both belong to a Minority group in the Sex game.

Today's movies bulge with Male pipe-dreams, gigantic heroes in the arenas of Studdery that boggle the imagination. Why, if one believes the movies even Woody Allen has a chance with Ursula Andress, and poor tired-eyed, weak-chinned Peter O'Toole is more effective than a red-eyed, short-tempered Durham bull among a herd of cows.

And what are the New Women doing during all this? Nothing. They don't have to. Now in the saddle, growing taller and heavier by the minute, they no longer need the fantasies and dreams of an earlier time.

The resident Husband now quietly mooning over the automatic washing machine, eyes glazing lustfully over Miss June, the Playmate of the Decade, his well-thumbed paperback edition of *The American Dream* by Norman Mailer in the back pocket of his lowcut saddle-stitched

Neo–Gary Cooper Levi's, waiting for the dryer to finish the week's laundry, his hands chafed and worn by long immersion in Mr. Clean, The Dishwater Wonder, uneasily fears the moment when Helen of Troy slams open the front door and bellows, "WHERE THE HELL'S SUPPER!!"

We are all in it together, and there is no turning back. The Great Role Reversal is rumbling upward and outward in an enormous mushroom cloud of irresistible force and all we can wait for now is the fallout and the casualty reports. A new age is dawning.

5

Confessions of a
TV Fisherman

EDITOR'S NOTE: Have you envied those
lucky devils who constantly appear on TV
outdoor specials fishing and hunting all
over the world, and in color: Rip Torn
shooting caribou; Robert Stack hunting everything; Bing Crosby popping away at
quail? How does it feel to be one of these
fortunate Showbiz outdoorsmen?

Jean Shepherd, *Field and Stream* con-
tributor and four-time *Playboy* Humor
Award winner, TV and radio performer
and avid although largely unsuccessful
fisherman caught Coho salmon in Lake
Michigan on CBS's "Fisherman's World"
last year. It was an exotic experience.

Upon being invited to go ice fishing by
the producer of "Fisherman's World" he
decided to keep a diary on just what it is
like to be a TV fisherman. He returned
from the Wisconsin hinterland with his tattered notebook: bourbon-stained and dog-
eared, his tackle box in one hand and the

latest copy of *Variety* in the other. He, for the first time in print, gives us the low-down on the fascinating and growing world of the Celebrity Sportsman.

January 16, 1972
[Written en route]
Boarded 727 United Airlines flight to Chicago at 7:50 p.m. Club Commuter flight. Just think, in a few hours I'll be out of this urban world of phony values and shallow attitudes and I will be in Wisconsin, where Life is real and Nature beckons.

I peer out of the plane window at long lines of airliners waiting for take-off in the miserable New York smog. Temperature 26 degrees. It is warm here in the First Class section. Behind us, in the rear of the plane, the grubby peasants in the Tourist section (steerage class) are already telling their lewd jokes; babies are crying, and old ladies complaining fitfully. Here in First Class all is serene. Well-fed ad men bound for Chicago and points West and god-knows-what chicanery surround me. We are up and away into the blackness, Manhattan receding below, a string of flickering Christmas tree lights scattered in the inky darkness.

By god, I'm lucky! There are probably forty million guys out there in Audienceland who would give damn near anything to go fishing on TV. I loll back in the soft vastness of my First Class seat, counting my blessings. I've come a long way from fishing for listless, suicidal crappies in Cedar Lake, Indiana, to the magnificence of CBS (full NET, in Color). Well, I deserve it. Fenton McHugh, the producer of "Fisherman's World," knows a good appealing characterful face when he sees one. There's one fly in the ointment, though.

Ah! The stewardess, a thin, nervous blonde, is passing out the drinkies. Two little green bottles of martinis and a corned beef sandwich. I feel a tiny glow of pleasure deep inside because I know they are paying for their drinkies back in Steerage. Let 'em eat cake, I say. The blighters are getting cheeky anyway. What the hell are these macadamia nuts anyway? I never heard of them before I started to fly First Class. They must have been invented by the airlines.

Two ad men in the seat ahead are getting noisy. They appear to be talking about TV. A third, wearing a Tom Jones shirt with tasteful plum and cerise stripes and a seven-inch-wide grape-colored tie that would have made a circus barker cringe, stands in the aisle, leaning over his two henchmen:

"Ed, the numbers boys tell you it's a buy. Don't argue. If it flops they can't hang you. After all, the numbers are what it's about, boy."

He slops a little vodka on the top of my head as the plane jiggles a bit in turbulence. If they only knew that a real TV star was sitting here, on top of it all, in mufti!

Oh yes, where was I? The fly in the ointment. The last time Fenton had me on TV I drew an assignment in colorful, exotic Manistee, Michigan, a town not without its rough-hewn, rustic charm, if you like diners and Shell stations, but certainly not one of the great watering places of the Western world. Now I'm en route to Lake Geneva, Wisconsin, and in mid-Winter! Why do other guys not half as cute as I am get sent to places like Bimini or the Andes, to fish for rare bugle-billed golden dudgeons while I have to settle for ice fishing for the usual minnows the Midwest fishermen have settled for for centuries? Oh well. Maybe you have to work up to the really great shows. Probably Robert Stack started out fishing with night crawlers for bullheads in an Ohio pay lake, on a black-and-white local show. Now look where he is, on all those African safaris, and hunting tigers with Maharajas.

My agent, his shifty eyes glowing with mendacity, his fake Viennese accent redolent of Seventh Avenue strudel, had yelped:

"Vell, ve are on our vay! Ve beat oud two musical comedy stars, a juggler from der Johnny Carson show und the lead guitar player for a rock group."

It is a choice part, a real plum.

It won't be long before we'll be in Chicago. I sip at my martini as I read over my typewritten instructions: *Meet Production Assistant at O'Hare. He will drive you to Playboy Club-Hotel at Lake Geneva. You should arrive at about 11:30 p.m. Fenton McHugh and John Bromfield, the show's host, will meet you there.*

The Playboy Club-Hotel! Ah yes, the fabled Xanadu of the Midwest barrens, a pleasure dome I've always wanted to see. Some say Kubla Khan himself drops by from time to time. We shall see.

The NO SMOKING sign is lit. We are slanting down through the overcast. Ah, Chicago, City of the Broad Shoulders, the 26 Girls, and my Youth.

[written in room 5308 Playboy Club-Hotel]

What have I gotten myself into? I'll recount the recent developments as coherently as possible.

I was met at the plane by Lee, the production assistant for Fenton McHugh. He seemed agitated and tense as we struggled through the crowds in the O'Hare terminal and out into the parking lot. It must have been a hundred degrees colder here in Chicago. The screaming wind swept over the parked cars, freezing the film on my eyeballs. I was home. The hated Midwest winters of my childhood came tumbling back.

We got out on the toll road, heading for Wisconsin, the frost creeping up over the windshield, snow swirling like a Sahara sandstorm over the hood.

"I've been having a hell of a time with those Bunnies."

"Yeah?" I muttered, too stunned by the cold to think straight. He pounded on the steering wheel.

"Just twenty-four hours ago me and the whole crew were in the Bahamas. And now this!" He scratched at the frost on the windshield ahead of him for a slight sliver of visibility.

"You were where?" I asked, not hearing

him well the first time due to an Arctic gale that was cracking through the car's insulation and down my neck.

"The Bahamas, dammit. Cat Cay."

God Damn it, I knew it! I might have been there!

"Who were you shooting with?" I asked.

"Boog Powell. He's some baseball player or something." I could see that Lee was not a rabid baseball fan.

"Didja ask him how come the Mets knocked them over like that in the Series?"

"Nah," was all he said as we pressed Northward, ever Northward into the howling gale. After a couple more toll houses his crack about the Bunnies soaked through the ice cube that had somehow mysteriously replaced my brain.

"What's that about the Bunnies?" I asked, shoving my feet deeper into the car's heater.

"Fenton thinks it'll be a great gag to have these Bunnies come out and serve you and John some stuff while you're fishing. You know, this joint is like a big Playboy club. They got all these Bunnies . . ." Lee trailed off thoughtfully.

"Bunnies? Serving us while we fish through the ice?" I have always heard of people's minds boggling. Up to that point mine never had.

"You know, Lee, this shooting might be more fun than I thought."

Lee snickered. "Don't bet on it, Dad. This Playboy outfit is stricter with these Bunnies than a nunnery."

"Oh well," I said, "there's always Blue-gills."

We wheeled on.

We had left the comparative civilization of Chicago far behind. Finally, the Lake Geneva turnoff loomed out of the snow-drifts and we headed toward the storied Playboy Club-Hotel, an establishment that is rarely mentioned in the effete East but which has become a major cultural shrine in what Colonel McCormick, the late, be-loved publisher of the *Chicago Tribune* used to lovingly call "Chicagoland." We were now on a two-lane road, threading our way through total blackness, the dark-ness that only a mid-Winter night in the Midwest can know. Lee hummed to him-self; I mused thoughtfully over the strange tricks that Showbiz had played on me.

Suddenly, there it was. Like some LSD apparition rising out of the deserted, snow-shrouded hills the fantastic, far-flung, Frank Lloyd Wright–inspired monument to the Good Life, its low-lying windows glowing warmly through the shifting snow; eerie Polynesian-style orange-blue flames flickering hotly before the stone entranceway, its gates guarded by a Security patrol that made the MPs at Fort Dix look like Cub Scouts.

"CBS!" Lee barked at the guard who had stopped our car. At this magic password the guard, his helmet gleaming darkly, saluted smartly and we were in.

What a sight! It at first reminded me of some vast, grounded stone dirigible lying sinisterly on a long, low, rolling hill, but no, more like a Mayan temple, a truly beautiful building of stone, flashing glass and dark, burnished bronze. As I climbed stiffly out of the Pontiac before the spectacular entranceway, a thought flashed through my mind: *My God, what hath Hefner wrought?*

Minutes later I was wandering through the corridors that sprawl on and on, looking for Room 5308 where I now sit, my plush apartment, black-leather-covered furniture and a vast floor-to-ceiling sliding glass wall opening on a balcony overlooking the whole state of Wisconsin. Five minutes later I am down in the Playroom, one of the innumerable nightclubs that

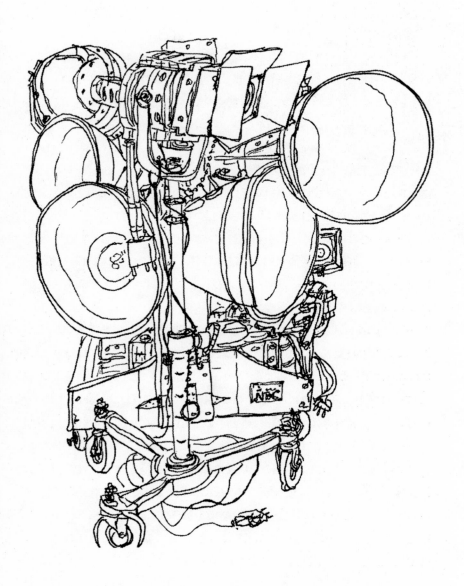

seem to go twenty-four hours a day: The Bunny Hutch, Man At His Leisure, The Cartoon Room. This is the way to go fishing!

"Hey boy, it's great to see you." Fenton rose from his table, his Showbiz boyish healthy face beaming with joviality and Grant's scotch.

"You're looking great, boy." He playfully belted me in the stomach. Up on the stage, a lady hypnotist with blinding blonde hair was brassily hypnotizing the audience.

"Good to see you, Fenton," I answered, still a little stunned by these wild sur- roundings. I thought I felt the Bends coming on.

"HEY, GANG!" Fenton shouted at his production crew who were scattered among the tables, ogling the passing Bunnies, their haunches jiggling as they toted potables (a favorite Playboy word) to the revelling key-holders.

"Shep here was with us in Manistee last Fall." He laughed wickedly, remembering the luxurious hotel we had stayed in on that one, a hostelry that Willy Loman would have found shoddy. A dapper char- acter wearing a blue cashmere sport coat and white turtleneck sweater, with opaque green sunglasses, sidled up. He had Hollywood written all over him.

"This is Jack, Shep. One of the best cameramen on the Coast." Jack, his glasses glinting mysteriously, cracked his tanned California face into a grin:

"What do you mean *one* of the best?"

I took off *my* sunglasses and answered: "Good to know you, Jack. How do you like this weather? It's probably rough on you California guys."

"These people don't live out here," he answered, "in fact I wonder if they are people. Hey Roy . . ." he called to his assistant, who was listlessly watching the hypnotist, ". . . here's a guy who takes off his sunglasses to say hello. Lets you see his eyes." He tapped me on the chest: "That's a compliment."

"Let's get away from the show." Fenton took charge.

"I want to talk over tomorrow's shooting." He herded us into another bar, the Living Room, where we sat around a huge table. John Bromfield joined us, looking slightly dazed.

"You were out for forty-five minutes. Do you know that?" Fenton rattled the ice cubes in his glass. "Knocked out colder than a mackerel."

"Oh come on." John looked dubious, far

less assured than he was when he was the U.S. Marshal on TV.

"Yeah, that hypnotist chick knocked you right out at the table. You put your head down and were gone for forty-five minutes."

John looked unconvinced. "Did I do anything bad or anything?"

"Nah. Just sat there looking stoned."

"I'll be damned!" Bromfield ordered a scotch and water. Introductions went around again and I instantly like Bromfield, a straightforward, open performer who really enjoys the Outdoors, completely virile, a rarity in the business, and a fine fisherman.

"Now look, we're shooting the kitchen scene at 8:00 a.m. Lee, I want you to put in a Cast Call at seven. John, you'll be working with the chef. We've got a scene on fancy ways to cook fish."

Fenton, an old friend of mine, is a born producer. He loves to bark out orders. For nine years he struggled to get the networks to do Outdoor shows, and at last they were beginning to see the light.

"Now Shep, you can sleep until nine o'clock or so because we won't be shooting with you until later."

"What am I going to do?" I asked, eager

to get at the ice fishing.

"You and John are gonna play a scene in the VIP Room. You gotta dress formal for this. These Bunnies we lined up are gonna serve you two guys the fish you caught. Prepared by the chef with wine and the works, before this roaring fire."

"You're not kidding, Fenton. This really ain't Manistee, is it?"

He laughed.

"Boy, do you remember that rubber steak we got, with those plastic French fries? That night after I caught the only fish, that six ounce Northern?"

"Well Shep, my boy, you will find the food is considerably better here. We're going First Class this time."

And no wonder. The first "Fisherman's World" featuring among other things the Coho sequence, Gypsy Rose Lee fishing for muskies, and Clare Conley, the editor of *Field and Stream* looking manly and rugged, had been not only a critical success but a smash in the ratings. It was one of two Nature specials to be nominated for an Emmy.

A rock group boomed thunderously from the Club next to the bar, totally wrecking conversation.

"Let's have another drink all around,

then get up to bed. We got a long day," Fenton bellowed as Bunny Sandy, her massive mammary structure inches from my eyes, took the orders. The Outdoors sure are a'changing.

January 18, 2:14 a.m.
[written as I soak in the tub]
How about that, Sports fans? This day reminded me of nothing so much as living through an avant-garde film made by a demented Swedish director. What a day!

For ten minutes after my wake-up call at 9:00 a.m. I staggered around the room trying to figure out where the hell I was. It is not easy to fully believe the Playboy Lake Geneva Taj Mahal when yanked out of a sound sleep. I spent the next half-hour lost in the maze of corridors, trying to figure out how to get to the ground floor where the complex of shops, restaurants, chi-chi boutiques specializing in fifty dollar slacks, twenty-five dollar shirts and fifteen dollar ties was located.

I finally found Fenton in the Living Room, sipping a cup of coffee before a vast panoramic window about the size of an up-ended tennis court. Outside, the chill white Wisconsin hills rolled to the horizon. The waitress poured my coffee. Hefner has

96

the decency not to hit you with Bunnies before martini time. I looked around, amazed at the motley crowd that occupied the other tables, as wholesome a gang of family types, complete with five-year-old children and motherly wives, as had ever taken out a subscription to *Reader's Digest* and went to a Billy Graham revival meeting.

"Hey Fenton, what is this? I thought this was a den of pure debauchery!"

"Shep, this place makes the Howard Johnsons look like a hotbed of depravity."

Elfin children darted about the room, chortling, just like they used to on the covers of the *Saturday Evening Post*. Moodily I sipped my coffee. Another illusion shattered. My Aunt Clara wouldn't have been out of place here, I thought.

Lee dashed up to our table, his eyes glinting brightly. In broad daylight he was pure Beaver, all bushy-tailed and eager.

"The chef wants to know if you want the vegetable plates shot separately or with the fish."

"Is John down there?"

"Yeah, and he's getting restless. Jack keeps changing the lights."

Fenton glanced at his watch. "They been on that scene for two hours! Have they got anything yet? Tell them I'll be right down."

Lee shot away, trailing smoke. We finished our coffee and Danish.

"Let's go down to the kitchen and get that chef on the stick."

We descended through the bowels of the vast complex down to the kitchen, a spectacular study in stainless steel, fluorescent lighting, radar ovens; one of the most modern plants I've ever seen. The chef, a short elfin Frenchman wearing a high Chef cap and what looked like a Doctor Kildare surgical coat, was arranging fish filets on a silver platter, garnished with parsley and shaved radishes. Jack, surrounded by his henchmen — a crowd of laconic, bearded revolutionaries — stood on a ladder adjusting a sinister-looking reflector that threw a peculiar yellow glow over the whole kitchen. Everywhere were cables, microphones, lights, and miscellaneous pieces of gear. In the midst of this complicated hodge-podge the chef looked like a tiny midget, lost and forlorn. John, his hair neatly combed, his make-up fresh and bronzed, sat on a frozen food chest. They had been working on the scene for some time now, it was obvious.

"Look John, don't mention what kind of fish it is," Fenton said to John. Like most producers he is a Jekyll and Hyde character who is completely jovial and in fact hilarious off the set but maniacally serious and involved when at work. He was working now.

"Don't worry," John said, as relaxed as ever, "it's going good."

"I don't want to even imply that these are the fish we caught. Let 'em think it, but I don't want us to say it."

"We already shot that scene," John said, "and it's fine. The cook didn't mention a thing."

The chef was ready. "How iss zees?"

I was astounded. He really was French. Jack squinted through his eyepiece.

"Move it just a shade to the left." Someone slid the tray a millimeter or so to the left.

"Hold it. Let's shoot."

Everyone instantly became silent and tense as the camera whirred, shooting close-ups of the tray of golden filets. Jack straightened up.

"Okay. Strike it." His green glasses glinted malevolently. A pro at work.

"Well, that's it for the kitchen scene." Lee, Fenton's assistant, was taking charge.

"Let's get set up in the VIP Room. That's gonna be a bugger." Jack, Roy, Billy and Lee banged around with the cases of equipment, knocking down the lights. The chef, no longer useful, had suddenly become invisible. He stood sadly by his fish, hoping someone would say something to him.

"That looks pretty good," I said, for want of anything better.

"Eet iss cold. She also iss cooked too much." He shrugged his shoulders in that special way Frenchmen have, radiating both disdain and confusion simultaneously.

"Look, Fenton, I gotta get a hat for my scene."

"Don't tell me you don't have that fantastic green hat you wore in the first show!"

"Dammit, Fenton, I was so rushed that I not only forgot my hat, I also forgot a spectacular scarf I have. Let's go into town. I gotta pick something up."

"Okay."

Fenton seemed glad to get away from the Playpen for a bit.

"While they're setting up in the VIP Room we can drive in to Lake Geneva."

An important part of these Outdoor shows is costuming. Every guy who does them regularly has his own style. Some wear African veldt hats, others go for Stetson ten-gallon jobs. Buckskin shirts, Indian beaded headbands; it's all part of the game. In the first "Fisherman's World" I had worn my favorite fishing hat, an Effanem Crusher made by Martin Cantor of Bangor, Maine. They are great hats and I wore mine with the side brims pinned up Australian style. It had been a smash hit on the show. It even got fan letters. I had stupidly left it at home. It was like Charlie Chaplin forgetting to bring his cane, or Groucho leaving his false mustache on the dresser. Without a costume an actor is just another walking-around Joe. Make no mistake. Everyone who works these Outdoor epics is an actor and had better have his costume ready. This show was in color, so I needed something that would really reach out of the screen and grab 'em. This is subtler than it sounds. You don't just pick up a red deer hunter cap or something ordinary that any straight fisherman would wear. It has to say something. Joe Foss without his hat would look like a tall insurance man.

We drove into town. Lake Geneva is really just one street; two rows of single story buildings and a lot of sky. Essentially a summer resort, in the winter it is almost a ghost town. The first place we went into had a magnificent six-foot orange and black fringed scarf. The instant I laid eyes on it I knew it was right. It would look good with my Spanish corduroy shooting jacket which I would wear over a turtle-neck hand-knit fisherman's sweater that I had picked up in the South of Portugal on another Showbiz jaunt.

"Y'got any hats?"

The clerk, a dead ringer for Harold Lloyd, looked blankly at the two of us, obviously non-Lake Geneva types.

"Just them stocking caps."

I glanced at them. Nothing.

We crossed the street to another place, more woodsy and hipper.

"Wouldja look at that, Fenton! *There's* the hat!" Marked down from ten dollars, a magnificent loden green Robin Hood style topper with a spectacular red and yellow feather grabbed me where I lived. I jammed it on my head.

"My god, you're right out of Charles Dickens!" Fenton laughed. "You look like Scrooge's partner."

I admired myself in the wavy mirror. With the orange and black scarf wound around my neck and billowing up to my eyes, my Robin Hood hat pulled low, I was ready for the color screen. There was also a shelf full of wild yellow and green stocking caps with big embroidered "Packers" badges on them. With a jolt it reminded me that I was back in the Midwest, where pro football is almost a religion. Packer fans look upon Chicago Bear addicts as infidels who need converting. Two stringy high school kids with lank blonde hair and that high-cheekboned look that you often see in the upper Great Lakes region watched surreptitiously as the two of us admired my hat. For an instant or two I thought there'd be trouble, but it passed. We drove back to the hotel. I felt better about the whole thing now. My costume gave me confidence.

Lunchtime. Do they ever feed around this joint! Like most professional film crews, drinking is fairly liberal, never to excess but just enough to keep the spirits up. A black bread/baked ham sandwich, with a slice of Bermuda onion. As we sat around the crowded dining room I could feel the curious eyes of the paying customers. Midwesterners never react to film crews the way Easterners do. Easterners always secretly hope to get in the movies and are always nosing around, showing you their teeth, hoping they'll get in a scene. Midwesterners pretend that they couldn't care less.

There wasn't much to do after lunch because the crew was laboriously setting up for the VIP scene. Starr, the hotel manager, a jovial giant with a Henry The Eighth fringe beard who breeds Morgan horses on his Wisconsin farm, shuffled around looking worried, with his little telephone call unit beeping constantly in his jacket pocket. There was a Bunny crisis and he was in the middle. The Bunny Mother (this is no joke; there *is* a Bunny Mother. There is even a Bunny Grandmother) had assigned girls other than the ones Fenton wanted to our scene because of "the schedule," whatever the hell that was. Apparently Bunnies live under an iron dictatorial system and they are assigned to jobs, like bomber crews. Starr was sweating profusely.

"We got these rules. I don't make 'em. They come from The Man himself."

Again he spoke earnestly into the telephone, amid the dining room hubbub. From time to time Lee would appear, his glasses glinting malevolently. Obviously the VIP scene was a bummer.

I knew better than to get involved. They would call me when I was needed. I wandered in and out of the maze of this fantastic resort. It really is like nothing I've ever seen, anywhere. I watched three spectacular girls and a skinny guy with knock-knees swimming in the wild, heated pool which is glass-enclosed and gives the impression of swimming amid the snowdrifts. All the while, unfortunately, in my mind was the nagging knowledge that I was not here for fun and games; was not part of the scene. It was just a job and I hoped it would go well. When you're seen coast to coast as a professional it changes things.

Time dragged by. John and I sat in the Cartoon Room looking at the snow, sipping hot chocolate. He reminisced about his old Hollywood friends; his life since he left South Bend, Indiana, as a boy. People working together get very friendly on these jobs.

"About 1963 I just decided I'd retire."

"That's pretty young to hang it up," I said.

"Oh, I don't know. After eight years of a TV series you get pretty tired. And anyway, I wanted to do more fishing. My wife felt the same way, so here I am."

He is now completely involved in Outdoor shows of one kind or another, because he loves doing them: the big

Sportsman's Show in Chicago, "Fisherman's World"; making appearances at trade shows. I told him about a Broadway play I was going into.

"I've never really done any Legit — a little Stock. It's too damn tough for me. Too much like work," he said.

It was beginning to get dark outside. Snow had begun to fall. The hills on the horizon were fading in the gray mist of winter twilight. We talked on.

"Okay, you guys. They're ready to shoot." From nowhere Fenton appeared, highly charged as he always gets during actual shooting.

"Let's get up there. They're about ready to go."

John and I hurried to our rooms to dress as formally as we could; ties, dark jackets. After all, this was the VIP Room.

I went down the hall to the room itself. They weren't actually using the VIP Room but had taken a suite and moved a few things about so that it looked exactly like the real thing. Inside the room, a fantastic tangle of cables, tripods, light banks; orange, red, blue, gold, white, made the room look like some Dr. Strangelove laboratory. Two Bunnies, Bunny Nancy, a tall, languid brunette, and Bunny Pert, a short wispy gamin, honey blonde and disturbingly intelligent, fussed with the special VIP Room table settings, which are absolutely unchangingly rigid. Great crystal goblets, heavy massive pewter dishes, glowing candlelight.

"Now look, girls. Pert, you're serving the fish. You move to Jean's left. Serve him first, and then move around the back of the table and serve John. Okay, guys. John, you sit on that side . . ." Fenton was in charge. ". . . You take the other, Shep. And cheat. Cheat left."

The crew milled about, eating peanuts. The sound man played with his huge earphones. Jack, always silent on the set, lurked in the background, his green glasses glowing in the candlelight.

"Hey, what the hell's with the white baby spot? We lost it." Jack glared around, looking for the light man. The sliding glass windows opening out on the balcony stood ajar. Outside on the balcony a glowing spot that had provided a highlight had somehow shifted position in the wind. All the while, I forgot to mention, a bitter Wisconsin glacial breeze blew through the voluptuous scene.

"Hey Billy, get that spot, baby."

The spot swung in the darkness.

"Hold it. That's it. Now lock it."

Jack peered through his viewfinder.

"Shep, you follow that spot. Can you find it?"

I nodded. The TV fisherman of today has got to know how to play the lights. He may not know a Royal Coachman from a Hawaiian Wiggler but he better know sight lines and amber spots or he isn't invited back.

"Nancy, you serve the wine. Y'got it, baby?"

Bunny Nancy smiled, her brilliant VIP Room velvet Bunny suit undulating. Bunnies wear special costumes in the VIP Room, purple velvet, sometimes dark red, trimmed in silver.

"Now look, baby, you show the wine to John, y'know, the label. Then pour a little in his glass. John, you sip it and nod. Got it?"

"What if I refuse it?"

John was playing for laughs.

"Then, Nancy, you come around the back of the table and pour some for Jean. Y'got it?"

Fenton, ever the master of dramatic scenes, was in the saddle. "Jean, John, are you guys listening?"

We weren't. We had been drifting off

into some inane gabble about the wine we were being served. Nancy was faking it by using an empty Coke bottle in rehearsal.

"Hey? Where's that ice bucket?" A note of alarm from Fenton.

"Oh no!!" Lee, a note of terror in his voice, rushed around the room looking for the ice bucket.

"I refuse to drink wine unless it is properly chilled. Even on TV," I quipped brilliantly.

Nobody laughed. This was costing about five-hundred-thousand dollars a minute, so every flubbed ice bucket meant more red ink. Finally everything was set. Silence descended on our tiny band of serious artists.

"All right, at my cue — Billy, you start the fireplace. Roy, hit the lights and we'll roll."

We all stood in position tensely, John and I seated like a pair of embalmed bon vivants amid sparkling glassware, the two Bunnies crouching nervously just out of camera range. Lee stood before us with his official-looking clapboard, slating the scene.

"VIP scene, shot one, take one."

CLAP! went the board. Clapboards actually do that. A faint hum filled the room

109

as the expensive color film whirred through the sprockets. The tape reels spun. Just out of camera range I could see the sound man hunching tensely over his V.U. meter.

"All right . . ."

Long pause.

"ACTION."

I felt Bunny Nancy moving up from behind. She undulated past my chair. I grinned up at her as she began to pour wine into John's glass.

"Hold it! Cut!"

We relaxed.

"Look, Honey, can you drop your shoulder? We got a fantastic shot of your shoulder."

Fenton injected kindliness into his voice in spite of the wasted film. Bunny Nancy looked a little nervous.

"Did I do it wrong?"

"No, honey. Just hold your left shoulder down when you pour. I know it doesn't feel natural, but it'll look right on the film."

She fiddled with the wine bottle. "Like this?"

"Okay. Fine. That looks a lot better. You ready, Jack?" Jack nodded. We went back to our places. John and I again faking casual Playboy sophistication, two Gentlemen at their Leisure. I straightened my tie.

"VIP scene, take two, shot one."

CLAP!

"ACTION."

Again Nancy snaked past as only a Bunny can. Gracefully she poured wine. John nodded approval. She circled the table. I grinned. She poured. She replaced the bottle in the ice bucket and drifted out. John and I raised our glasses in a toast.

"Beautiful. Wrap it up. Great." Fenton beamed.

A few lights were shifted. I watched Bunny Pert re-arrange her spectacular tray of fish. Since the fish had been cooked hours before, they looked great but were about as edible as Palmolive soap. Garnished with sprays of parsley and potato rosettes, they would look luscious on screen. I felt my stomach growling. It had been a long time since that black bread sandwich and all this pretending to eat had started the juices flowing.

"Now remember, Pert, serve Jean first. Nod to him and then serve John. Now watch your shoulder."

"VIP scene, shot two, take one."

CLAP!

It was a fiasco.

"Fer Chrissake, where's that rock band coming from?" The sound man was picking up extra sounds. None of us could hear it.

"Shh!!" He held up his hand for silence as he concentrated on listening to the ear-phones.

"They stopped." The phantom rock band apparently was just tuning up some-where.

"VIP scene, shot two, take two." CLAP!

Bunny Pert, her gamin face lit with an incandescent smile, laid an icy slab of fish on my plate. I grinned dumbly at it; trying to look elegant as across the table John was doing likewise. Behind me the gas fireplace roared menacingly. It wouldn't look right in the scene if my coat was on fire. This could turn into a Marx Brothers picture very easily.

"Beautiful, beautiful. Wrap it up!"

Art had triumphed again.

"Okay, gang, all I need now is a couple of reaction shots. We'll take you, John, first." Jack and his minions focused the camera full-face close-up on John.

"Shep, you sit out of range and give him something to react to."

Again the clapboard routine. John

smiled casually into the camera, a grizzled pro, something he had done into countless lenses.

"Wrap it up. John, give Shep something to work on." We reversed places. This time the faint blue glittering lens focused on me. CLAP!

My lip curled casually, a man enjoying a fish dinner amid Bunnies. I, too, have faced many a camera. I turned my Cute face on, full camera.

"Beautiful. Wrap it up. Strike it, boys. That's it. That went real good."

The VIP scene was over, a full day's work for a crew; actors, cameramen, Bunnies. God knows how much it cost. It would last maybe forty-five seconds on screen and would look so easy, so natural.

We went downstairs to the Living Room again. By now I had no taste for fish. I had a steak. John ordered ribs. Fenton had London Broil. By unwritten protocol the crew eats at a different table from the producer and stars. A deafening rock band made conversation impossible. We shouted back and forth for a while but our heart wasn't in it. It had been a tough day. Outside, the temperature was dropping. It was now near zero and as black as the inside of your hat, but here in the Playboy Hotel it

was all golden and warm and totally af-
fluent. John went up to bed. Fenton and I
lingered for a while and then called it a
day. For some reason I was tired. Tomorrow will be a real bummer, to use
Lee's phrase, especially in this cold.
They're calling me at 6:30 a.m. That
means maybe four hours of sleep. I'd better
grab 'em.

January 19, 1972 10:40 p.m.
[written aboard United Airlines 727 flight
Chi./NY]
Never again will I consider ice fishing a
sport that real human beings indulge in.
Masochists, yes. Idiots training to join Na-
poleon's retreat from Moscow, yes. Guys
writing books who want to experience
first-hand what the Panzer divisions went
through in the frozen wastes of Mother
Russia, yes. As for me, if dem warm
breezes ain't blowin', old Dad is gonna get
all the fish he needs at the nearest A & P.
I should have known, after that night-
mare. What a buster! I had this dream
where I was trying to buy a ticket at the
box office that they had set up next to a
trout stream in Montana. There were two
hundred thousand wildly cheering fans in
the stands, watching Elvis Presley and Bob

Hope fish for rainbows while Fred Mc-Murray played the saxophone. I couldn't get a ticket. It was sold out, and the next thing I knew I was trying to climb under the fence at this stadium they had built entirely around a North Woods lake, where the cast of *Oh! Calcutta!* was fishing for Northerns from red, white and blue kayaks. They were in costume, and it was being televised by Telstar around the globe, on some show called "Interplanetary Sportsman," choreographed by Gene Kelly, with an original score by Henry Mancini. A giant neon-encrusted blimp sailed overhead, emblazoned:

ROONE ARLEDGE PRESENTS

Just at the point when the cast, in costume, was singing a salute to Curt Gowdy to the tune of "Old Black Joe" I woke up in a cold sweat. For a minute I lay there not sure whether it was a dream or not. After all, I was about to go ice fishing with a couple of Bunnies and a TV Marshal.

During the night the temperature had dropped to around zero and a steady snow was falling, causing camera problems. After a breakfast of scrambled eggs done Playboy style, which naturally includes vast copper pots and twenty-seven different varieties of muffin. Playboys live good. They lounged all about the place, Kenosha shoe salesmen and Green Bay insurance men, a speedy lot.

Fenton was dressed in an exceedingly expensive Abercrombie & Fitch style cowled Arctic coat. It seemed designed for film directors. Unfortunately he didn't know how to work the complicated belt buckle, but that was only incidental to the dashing hood, which was more photogenic than practical.

John wore earmuffs and a dogged look. His heart was still in the Bahamas, but his backside was in Wisconsin. I pulled my Robin Hood hat down over my ears, wound my scarf around my neck and we waddled out into the bracing atmosphere of the tundras, which we would battle through a long, miserable, numbing day.

Jack had set his camera on the highest balcony of the hotel, pointed out at the distant hills. Below the hotel the land angled steeply away to a great hollow, at the bottom of which is a man-made pond. There are no houses, telephone poles, or signs of habitation to be seen from the balcony, just a great valley of snow, dotted with sharply-etched black trees right out of

116

a Japanese print. A steady 18 mph wind out of the North set the snow swirling in rolling clouds. Jack was excited by the desolation and beauty he saw through his viewfinder. He hopped up and down and slapped his hands together, his green sunglasses dotted with snow flakes.

"Look, they make real stars!" He was from California, and like many members of primitive tropical tribes, he had never seen snow.

"Yes they do, Jack, and when you get a lot of those stars piled up you can make a snowman, Jack, or even roll a Bunny in the snow."

He couldn't get over the snow flakes. He kept looking at one that was stuck on the end of his thumb. It was so cold our breath hung steadily in the air. A tall, thin, weatherbeaten man, beanpole rather, right out of Central Casting plodded up the hill, wearing a dark green Arctic thermal suit. It was Slim Lechner, "Fishing Technical Advisor" on our expedition, operator of the Fox River Bait Store and classic Midwestern outdoorsman. He was instantly likeable, a born Pfc. which in fact he was.

"Yep, I was a private for two and a half years, which ain't easy to manage," he told me when we began reminiscing about the

Army. "They only made me a Pfc. 'cause they put out some rule that they hadda give you a stripe when you went overseas."

"You didn't start throwing your rank around then, Slim, did you?" I asked.

"Naw, I demanded respect, but I wasn't too hard on the boys."

"We're gonna open with a Doctor Zhivago shot, with a vast Arctic scene of snow," Fenton explained the scene to John and me while Slim shifted from foot to foot in the snow.

"Now this is gonna be the first thing they'll see on the screen. They got no idea that you guys are fishing at the Playboy Club. We come right out of the Bahama sequence into this scene that looks like it could be Greenland or some place. We see two tiny figures struggling through the snow, just two dots, y'got it?"

We nodded, blowing steam in great clouds. It really would be a spectacular sight on a color TV set. It was genuinely a good idea.

"Then we cut to you two guys actually fishing and the audience meets you, Shep. You are showing John how a hip fisherman operates, first class. He doesn't know that you are at the Playboy Club. Neither does the audience, and then, suddenly, out of

118

the snow, come these Bunnies serving you coffee with rum in it. John is amazed, but you play it cool because that's the way you live. Okay?"

Slim grinned at this Showbiz talk. Ten minutes later John and I alone, pulling a sled behind us with our "gear," were far out down the valley, in knee-deep snow, tracking through virgin drifts, getting colder by the second. A half mile away, the cameras ground.

"You fall down, Shep, and I'll reach down and drag you out of the snow."

I flopped over sideways, my arms flailing like semaphores. Snow trickled down my neck. John reached down and grabbed my scarf, dragging me to my feet. We pretended to struggle forward. He stumbled and fell headlong. I reached down and pulled him to his feet and the two of us, bowing into the wind (which was real, very real) tottered onward, dragging our little sled behind. Through the sigh of the wind a distant shout drifted down into the valley. It was Fenton, letting us know the scene had been shot.

"Fantastic! You guys looked like something right out of the frozen Yukon, like the Mounties were after you."

"My god, is it cold!"

John blew his nose into a mitten. Icicles hung from the brim of my Robin Hood hat. This job was rapidly ceasing to be fun. We trudged on down to the site they had set up on the surface of the pond where we were to "ice fish." As a gag Fenton had had the crew lay a red carpet on the ice. Two holes had been bored through the ice and through the carpet. We were to fish through a red carpet for elegance. Behind us, a two-man green pop tent leaned into the wind. A table and two chairs on the red carpet was where we would play out our dramatic scene.

Now began the process of delay, backing and filling, bitching, recrimination, and total boredom that accompanies every shooting sequence in the film world, whether it is a monster Biblical epic or an innocent one-minute commercial for disposable baby diapers. It is this predictable yet unavoidable period which causes film stars to take up all manner of vice, from heady gambling sprees in Las Vegas to forays into politics. The intense boredom that a performer feels while the crew battles endlessly the elements and the equipment, while delay piles upon delay until there is nothing left but a dull buzzing in the head as the hours meander by, can be tolerated, but barely, in the confines of a warm studio, even mildly enjoyed when shooting in the tropics; but this day on the ice at the pond within snowball range of the most luxurious pleasure dome in the country it became sheer frigid torture.

First the camera froze solid. Then the heater which had been brought down from the hotel refused to work. The wind was causing bad noises in the sound man's earphones, and the holes which had been cut in the ice for fishing kept freezing over. The camera was wearing what looked like a little Arctic parka, under which Jack would peek from time to time, swearing delicately. Roy, his assistant, fiddled with the cables. John and I sat at the table, pretending to fish, rehearsing our lines.

"I GOT IT!" Jack shouted into the howling gale. "WE GOTTA GET WARM FILM CARTRIDGES AND SHOOT BEFORE THEY FREEZE UP."

It was the cartridges and not the camera that were causing us trouble, apparently, so a party was sent up to the hotel to get cartridges. We were using a big Johnson Sno Horse which roared up and down constantly, sending up clouds of fine snow. We were racing against time, as the Wisconsin January night comes on fast. We still had no clear idea of what to say or do on screen, even if the camera did work.

Simultaneously all three of us, John, Fenton and myself, arrived at a "Story line." The camera would open on John fishing alone. He would call me out of the tent. After introducing me, I would appear, sit down, and we would have a short, snappy scene. This was Take One.

"Let's go, you guys, before this magazine freezes up. It's working!"

Roy and Jack huddled over the camera protectively. I crouched in the icy tent which was loaded with film cans, reflectors, spare cables and props for the next scene. This would, of course, not be visible to the audience. Slim had set up our fishing gear, complete with tip-ups and tiny ice bobbers. Fenton took charge.

"You guys know what you're gonna do, now," he shouted, "let's go. Slate it."

Lee popped up with his board. Meantime, I crouched in the tent, waiting for my cue. My nose began to run from the cold. The tent flapped and groaned all around me. I heard the clapboard distantly, and then silence. Then came my cue:

"Jean, Jean! . . ."

I stuck my head out of the tent, as we had rehearsed.

"What do you want?"

John swung his arm toward me. I left the tent and trotted across the ice, conscious of the camera and the crew lurking about tensely. They were as tired of the frozen North as I was and wanted to see it over and done. I squatted on my icy chair. The dialogue began:

SHEP: "How you doing, John baby? Any action?"

JOHN: "Nothing." (He peers at bobber disgustedly.)

SHEP: "No wonder. They're not due here yet." (delivered with look of superior knowledge, an on-top-of-it look)

JOHN: (looking up, look of confusion) "What do you mean they're not due yet?"

SHEP: (chuckling in superior fashion) "Look, John, a gentleman doesn't waste his time fishing when there are no fish around. Fish only appear when action is imminent."

JOHN: "But how do you know . . . ?"

SHEP: "Don't worry. I know. Just watch your bobber. They're about due."

JOHN: (in amazement) "Well I'll be

darned! I've got one!" (His bobber dips. He struggles with a fish. Shep watches in satisfaction.)

JOHN: "Well what do you know! A catfish!" (He pulls catfish out of hole. Catfish had previously been attached to line by Slim Lechner, who took it out of a tank for that purpose.)

JOHN: (holding up fish delightedly) "How do you like that, a catfish!"

SHEP: "It's a bullhead." (He snorts.)

JOHN: "What do you mean, a bullhead? It's a catfish!"

SHEP: (laughing) "It's a bullhead."

JOHN: (holding up fish so camera can catch it) "Let me tell you, they're mighty fine eating."

SHEP: (in close-up, lip curling sardonically) "John, a gentleman does not fish merely to eat." (John does take; looks at Shep with reproach.)

SHEP: "Oops! Well what do you know." (He hauls out Bluegill.)

SHEP: "Now there, John, is an elegant fish. Notice the subtle coloring. Inch for inch this is the most fighting fish found in the fresh waters of America." (Shep drips superiority, holding fish in palm of hand for camera.)

JOHN: "Yep." (Playing Simple Good-guy role to the hilt.) "It shor is. Let me tell you, though, I'm really cold. It was a struggle getting up here. I could use something hot. . . ."

SHEP: "Ah yes. It shouldn't be too long now." (Shep glances at watch mysteriously.)

JOHN: (in astonishment) "What do you mean, shouldn't be too long?"

SHEP: "Just be patient." (He looks over John's shoulder into distance.)

SHEP: "Ah, yes. Here they come now!" (John turns head to look in direction Shep indicates. Jaw drops in astonishment.)

END OF SCENE

Amazingly, it went off like clockwork. Even the crew laughed at our frigid buffoonery.

"WRAP IT UP. PUT IT AWAY!" Fenton shouted in delight. In quick succession we shot two "reaction" shots, close-ups, of my face listening to John and his face listening to me. These would be intercut in the final version. The now frozen fish lay at our feet forgotten, their job done, forever immortalized on film.

Two Bunnies had been brought from the hotel by Sno-Horse and they clung together in the tent. They were central to the next scene. Bunny Bonnie and Bunny Moe, looking almost identical in their coats and boots, their black velvet bunny ears flapping in the Arctic wind. Incidentally, Bunnies never have last names and, in fact, many of the Bunnies have aggressively masculine first names: Bunny Sam, Bunny Lenny, even Bunny Irving. I will leave this manifestation to psychologists to ponder.

I stuck my head in the tent and introduced myself. The two Bunnies grinned in spite of their chattering teeth. Bunnies are creatures of the Indoor life.

"What are you guys supposed to be doing?" Bunny Moe asked.

"Fishing through the ice," I answered as I crept into the tent with them. John's head appeared through the flap, blowing steam.

"I gotta get in! I'm freezing!" He crawled in. There were now four of us in a tent designed for two small Cub Scouts (vertical).

"Gee, are you guys on TV?" Bunny Bonnie, who looked a little like old Lauren Bacall stills, said with what I was sure was a put-on.

"Yeah," John answered, fishing out a cigarette from among his sweaters. This sparkling conversation continued for several minutes. Bunnies are meant to be seen, not heard. They were cute, though, like kittens or something. They radiate a strange aura of perpetual Senior Prom-ishness even in the snow. The snowmobile roared outside the tent. Lee's head shoved its way into our tightly knit group.

"Let's go, girls. I want to shoot you in the snowmobile." For the next fifteen minutes the girls roared back and forth in front of the camera, Bunny Bonnie expertly piloting the snowmobile while Bunny Moe waved from behind.

The time had arrived for our next big scene. It began where the last scene had ended, with John's amazed look.

"Okay, let's slate it." Lee clapped his trusty clapper. A fresh, warm film magazine began to turn. For an instant a thought flashed through my mind: *What the hell is this all about, anyway? We're grown-up people!*

The Bunnies, wearing fur boots, their velvet ears outlined sharply against the white hills, ambled into camera range, carrying silver trays with prop pewter mugs and dishes of mixed nuts, napkins and silverware.

BUNNY MOE: (to me, placing mug before me) "I'm your Bunny, Bunny Moe."

ME: (grinning foolishly) "Yessiree. Hello, Bunny Moe."

BUNNY BONNIE: (to John, placing mug before him) "I'm your Bunny, Bunny Bonnie."

JOHN: (picking up mug) "Thank you, Bunny Bonnie." (John looks at me in amazement, unaccustomed to such elegance while ice fishing.)

ME: "This is the way to fish. This is the way a gentleman ice fishes."

JOHN: "You're right! This is more like it!" (We clank mugs.)

ME: "Say, how do you like this hat?"

JOHN: "Hat?"

ME: (assuming superior air) "This hat is the escutcheon of the most exclusive fly-tying club in the Scottish Highlands." (John snorts in disgust, glances at my bobber.)

JOHN: "Yeah? Well, put another worm on; you're cleaned." (I do a take, first at him, then down at my cleaned hook.)

The crew laughed in appreciation. Only one thing was wrong. During the shooting some kids on the distant toboggan slope began shouting, at just the wrong moment.

We played the scene over, the Bunnies' noses a little redder than before. This time it worked.

"Great! Wrap it up! It's in the can." Fenton clapped his mittens together. The great ice fishing scene was over. It was all up to the cutting room now.

Bunny Bonnie appeared at my right. "My tail is gone," she said mournfully, with a touch of fear in her voice. Even though I was half frozen I was still capable of faint surprise.

"My tail blew away." Sure enough, her big fluffy white cottontail had blown off and was now rolling down the ice a quarter of a mile away.

"Never fear, Bunny Bonnie, I'll rescue your tail." Gallantly I slipped and slid over the rough pond ice, chasing Bunny Bonnie's tail. I thought: *Too bad they couldn't film this scene. Now this is what I call Hunting!*

Twenty minutes later we were all back up in the hotel. John was upstairs in his room, on the phone to Chicago, and left almost immediately for a rehearsal of his big Sportsman show that was opening the next week. The tight-knit camaraderie of our little unit was rapidly dissolving. We were beginning to be strangers again who would probably never see each other until professional chance might throw us together. Jack was busy in the tailor shop buying a Swiss knit suit. Lee had disappeared with his clipboard. I never saw him again.

I sat in the Cartoon Room drinking hot chocolate with Bunny Moe and Bunny Bonnie, making small talk. They got up and left. I went upstairs and packed. Dinner that night was somewhat strained and hurried. We were all anxious to be on our separate ways. Fenton drove me to O'Hare through the beautiful Wisconsin countryside. We talked about a feature he was planning and decided to meet in New York two weeks hence and discuss it further. O'Hare is a cold airport with a keening wind sweeping out of the prairies with a steady monotonous beat. Luckily I got a plane earlier than I'd planned.

Back in good old First Class, among the sleek, well-fed Expense Account people. I wondered for a moment whether Slim even suspected they existed, or whether any of them could have imagined the Aquarium Lounge that Slim did business with. He had said:

"Yep, I seine my minnows out of the Fox River."

"Yeah," I said, "but how do you get along in the winter? There aren't many fishermen."

"Well, I do all right," he answered solemnly. "I supply the Aquarium Lounge with minnows."

"You do?" I was surprised. "What do they do with minnows at the Aquarium Lounge?"

"They got an aquarium on the bar. And these guys come in and scoop up shiner minnows with their hand and swallow 'em. They wash 'em down with beer."

"They swallow 'em? Live?" I was astounded.

"Yep," Slim answered matter-of-factly. "And other people come in and sit in the booths and watch 'em."

I could imagine the scene! Again my mind boggled, for the second time in two days.

"Is that the biggest show in town, Slim?"

Slim detected my sarcasm.

"Well, you ain't never seen 'em."

As the tray of Martinis and the inevitable macadamia nuts were passed before me in the warm, comfortable glow of First Class, I reconsidered. Yep, that probably would make a good act on the Dick Cavett Show, the boys swallowing mud minnows Coast to Coast and washing them down with the sponsor's beer. The crowd would love it. Probably up Cavett's rating, too. At least in the Midwest. I wonder how our little act will go over? Maybe next time I'll draw Bimini. Who knows?

6

Harold's Super Service

There are nights when I'm driving my Fiat 124 along the turnpike and I've got the radio set way down near the end of the dial where the Cuban and the Puerto Rican stations come fading in and I'll pick up WWVA in Wheeling. I'll be driving along in the dark, along the pike, and there, drifting through the birdies and harmonics of the ghetto end of the radio dial, the sad, mournful wail of Merle Haggard sings about that good ol' boy pumping gas at Harold's Super Service. Sometimes Merle barely makes it through the hellfire and damnation barrage being laid down by Oral Roberts on a station riding right in under WWVA.

Last night I dreamed I died and went to Heaven . . .
To that mighty Super Service in the sky.

Harold's Super Service is a country-western song about a guy pumpin' gas at a place that specializes in "service all the way." But there's one thing that bugs him; this guy that shows up in a "stripped-down Model A" who demands: "Gimme fifty cents worth a'reg'lar, check the oil too, if you don't mind, put some air in my tires would ya mister? . . . and wash my windows too when you get time." Well, it seems that when this pump jockey dreams he died, he was quite happy in the great bye-and-bye. His pump was right near the Pearly Gates, where he could see the new arrivals check in every day. He was happy pumping gas throughout all Eternity, when one day, as he was changing the plugs on Moses' magic carpet, who shows up chuggin' through the clouds but that big old boy in his stripped-down Model A. "Gimme fifty cents worth a'reg'lar. . . ."

I don't know whether Haggard ever pumped gas in his life, but as a guy who once, in his fifteenth year, spent four hellish weeks pumping Esso in a sun-baked pit stop on US 41 in the shimmering heat of an Indiana summer, I know well what the poor son-of-a-bitch in Harold's means.

An afternoon in the grease pit, draining scalding oil out of the guts of GMC tractors while the rest of the world sings and dances all about you, is enough to put the good old iron in anyone's soul. Sometimes I watch those Amoco or Shell commercials on TV with that legion of square-jawed, trimly-uniformed, sparkling-eyed attendants briskly shining windows and polishing headlights on an endless succession of what appear to be showroom models, and think about the times I was alone at that station. Elmer Lightfoot, who owned the station, was off making it with the blonde. And there I'd be, left with those goddamn pumps, and the ultimate cross: the grease rack.

Elmer, on those days when the blonde was in season and he was coming into rut, and her old man was in Logansport trying to peddle pianos or bugles or whatever the hell it was he sold, would say to me about 10:30 in the morning: "Well, she's all yours, kid."

He'd toss me the keys to the register and take off in his bored-out, chopped-down, high-assed Hudson Hornet which he raced at Crown Point on the weekends. That Hornet was so mean that it'd sit out there in the back, with the key off, burnin' rubber standing still. In fact, that Hornet was a lot like Elmer himself. You know the old crap about how people who own dogs get to resemble their mutts. Well, I think

135

cars are even more so. Square-looking chunky guys who wear white-on-white ties always buy square-looking chunky Chryslers, and Elmer was a lot like his Hudson Hornet; ugly, hard to handle, and at times as mean as cat dung. And as he rocketed off to his tryst, Elmer would scream out the window, "Keep an eye on it, kid, and WATCH THEM CRAPPERS! I don't want no winos from Cal City boozin' it up in there, y'hear?"

"Yeah, Elmer," was all I could say, because he was right. The first time I had been left in charge, this guy had come in driving a Studebaker Champ with the back stove in and the windows held together with white adhesive tape. He fell out of the car while I was trying to fish out the rag he had been using as a gas cap. I gave him the keys to the john, and three hours later we had to call the Sheriff to bust down the door and drag him out, drunk as a skunk. For the rest of the day I mopped up vomit and tried to get the plumbing working again.

"Okay, Elmer, I'll watch it."

There was one day in particular that sticks in my memory as exactly what old Merle means. As usual, the Hudson had left me standing there in the heat amid clouds of blue exhaust and burnt rubber. I hadn't had anything to eat since six that morning and my stomach was growling like a flat head Ford about to lose its main bearings, so the first thing I did was look for something to eat. All I could come up with was a Butterfinger which was under the counter where Elmer had his leather-covered jack handle, in case of trouble. He had covered the thing in cowhide himself, with neat stitching and his name burned on it in fancy lettering. Elmer said he learned leathercraft in the Scouts, and "it come in handy when you're makin' a blackjack." He also kept a .38 Police Special stuck in the back of the shelf, under some rags, but I never saw him do anything with it except to take it out once in a while and show it to friends of his from the softball team. He mentioned it to me once.

"See this, kid. Won it in a raffle in Muncie. Bought this ticket from a guy in a bowling alley and doggone if I didn't win. Shows you never can tell."

He could spin it on his finger like Gary Cooper, and once it flew off and busted the mirror on the cigarette machine, which made Calvin the cigarette man mad and Elmer had to buy a new mirror. He didn't play with it after that, except he did show it off now and again. He never said whether it had shells in it or not, but knowing Elmer it must have had.

After Elmer left me with the key and nothing to do but wait for trouble to drive in and squirt Flit at the bluebottle flies and the hornets which kept coming in to the office to get out of the heat, I squatted down at Elmer's desk, wearing my Esso cap square on my head, and tried to look official.

Elmer kept his library — for dull moments between grease jobs — in the bottom drawer, along with a couple of Salvation Army coffee mugs and a jar of mustard. He never changed the books as long as I was there, and he never got tired of reading them. There was the July issue of *Spicy Western*, which featured pornography on the range, where there is never a discouraging word, to say the least; three little blue books graphically detailing the sexual adventures of Maggie and Jiggs, Winnie Winkle and Tillie The Toiler, a Western Auto catalog; and the National League Yearbook, which was referred to constantly during heated arguments on Saturday mornings with his friend Swifty and a guy named Leo who sold grease fittings.

Well, I sat there for a while reading *Spicy Western* and this story about a guy named Luke who had this pinto horse named "Paint," and one day he and Paint got caught in this bad thunderstorm and they had to spend the night in a deserted cabin with this strange girl who came galloping in out of the rain, and Luke got to sweating and wondering about whether her mammoth bazooms were going to pop right through her leather jacket, when somebody started to honk out by the gas pumps.

I picked up a rag, which most pump jockeys carry around like Linus' security blanket, and drifted out into the heat waves to go to work. It was a bile-green Oldsmobile. Back then, I was convinced that someone at the Olds plant was either color-blind or had a sneakily malevolent sense of humor in foisting those curiously depressing colors off on the public. This one was in that metallic bile color so favored by the same crew that loads up its lawns with concrete nymphs and plastic ducks. The Olds was piled high with luggage, topped by a green canoe with an Indian head on the bow.

"What'll it be?" I said out of the corner of my mouth, aping Elmer who at that

139

time was the model for my life style. Elmer had at least thirty-four variations of "What'll it be?," ranging all the way from mewling servility to an out-right challenge to a bloody fistfight. It was all in the tone of the voice and the way you wore the bill of your cap.

"Uh . . . do you have any Kentucky maps?" The driver, obviously Daddy, sweating as he struggled to open the door, his red plaid sport shirt rumpled and dripping, bunched up around his neck like a soggy noose. His wife, a thin wiry lady in a pink-flowered housedress, swatted at a wrestling mob of greasy kids in the back seat with a tennis shoe.

"Now stop it!" she yelled. "I SAID STOP IT!" She slugged away at the moiling mass.

"Y'got a map of Kentucky?" The old man battled free from his screaming brood.

"Kentucky?" I asked, stalling for time since I knew what all grizzled pump jockeys know, that when a guy asks for a map *and* gets out of the car it's nothing but trouble . . . and no sale. I started back toward the office to get him his Kentucky map when the back door of the Olds slammed open and three grubby kids wearing Popeye T-shirts and carrying rubber daggers poured out, yelling. The tar on the driveway was so hot I could feel my feet sinking in, and the smell of used oil made my eyes water as I grubbled through our supply of maps.

"How 'bout West Virginia?" I asked.

"We're heading to Corbin. I gotta have a Kentucky map," was all he said, mopping away at his sweating forehead.

"I got an Ohio map that shows part of Kentucky, but that's all. We run out of Kentuckys."

"Fer Chrissake, what kinda station is this? No Kentucky maps!"

"All I got's Ohio." Behind me I could hear the kids flushing the john over and over, and squirting water around the walls.

In the meantime a Pontiac convertible and a Chevy station wagon had pulled in and begun to honk.

"I'll be right back!" I hollered at the Kentucky traveler. The girl in the Pontiac wanted to know what that squeak was up in the front . . . and if Elmer was going to be around.

"It's probably your fan belt," I yelled above the din of Route 41 traffic and screaming kids. The guy behind her in the Chevy was putting out so much steam that it looked like any minute he'd blow his hood clean off.

"Hey, I'm heating up!" he bellowed.

The girl kept gunning her motor, trying to make it squeak. The guy who wanted the Kentucky map was now in the office, rummaging through Elmer's desk where he kept his Winnie Winkle books. It was getting out of hand, going downhill fast. I ran back into the office and shoved an Ohio map at the bird in the plaid shirt.

"We only got Ohio maps!" I could see he was already halfway through Tillie The Toiler and couldn't care less. Thank God, his wife started to toot.

"Your wife's tooting."

"Yeah, I know." He sounded mad. He clutched the Ohio map and herded the kids back into the car. They were playing soccer with a wad of rolled-up paper towels. He finally cleared the driveway and headed for Corbin, Kentucky.

In the meantime the girl with the Pontiac had driven off in the direction of the Shell station, and good enough for 'em, I thought. The Chevy, in the meantime, had all but exploded.

"TURN IT OFF!" I hollered through the roar of escaping steam.

"What?" The driver, for some reason,

kept racing the engine.

"TURN IT OFF!" I yelled. He cut the switch, and that damn Chevy was so hot she kept running for five minutes on self-combustion alone. I saw the guy behind the wheel was some kind of minister or something. He had one of those reverse collars and a black suit, and again I knew from experience that this was bad news. Preachers hardly ever buy more than three gallons of regular and tend to sponge a lot, figuring the Lord, and Jersey Standard, will provide. I finally got the hood open, and sheets of searing heat curled my eyelashes.

"It's empty. How come you didn't put no water in it?" I asked, peering into the radiator, which was coughing and panting faintly, and seemed to be crying.

"Water?" the preacher asked, as if he were above such mundane, earthly considerations as water in the radiator.

"Yeah, it's empty, fer Chrissake." The words got out before I could stop it.

"Excuse me, son?"

"It needs water. We'd better let it cool off, 'cause if I put water in it now she'll crack a block or something."

"Very interesting." The preacher gazed around the premises with the serenity of

143

the man who habitually leaves the scut of life to the others.

A kid on a Harley boomed down to the end pump. I sold him 1.3 gallons of High Test and a half pint of upperlube, a total sale of a buck thirty-seven and I'd been toiling, totin' barges and liftin' bales for over three hours and the day was just starting. I got back to the minister, who somehow didn't seem to sweat. He asked me what church I went to and before I could answer a guy in a Chrysler Imperial steamed in and asked if I knew where he could get a used generator. I said I didn't know, but I'd keep it in mind, which was a lie, and he drove out, leaving a trail of oil on the driveway. The minister gave me a tract entitled "Are You Prepared To Meet Thy Maker?" which he said was very interesting and could change my life forever. I filled the Chevy up with water, screwed the cap back on and he said, "Thank you, my son," got in and drove off.

After that it was quiet for a while. I went back and started to read about Luke and old Paint when the Coke man drove in and asked how come Elmer hadn't left the money for him and why were we short eight empties in one of the cases? I said I didn't know, but I'd ask Elmer, so he said

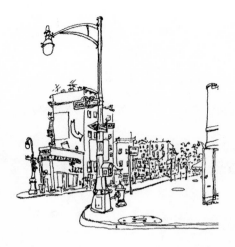

he wasn't gonna leave no Coke unless he got his money, unplugged the machine and drove off.

I figured it was no skin off my nose, so I sat down again, waiting for more action. A Scoutmaster drove in with an open-bodied vegetable truck loaded with Cub Scouts wearing baseball suits.

"How do I get to Black Oak?" he asked.

"You mean over by Griffith?" I asked. He said yeah. I told him and off they went. Another big deal. All the while it was getting hotter. My stomach was growling even more. When the Good Humor man came in to use the john I bought a Raspberry Swirl fudgesickle from him and he drove out, ringing his bell.

The phone rang. It was Elmer.

"How's everything goin', kid?"

"Okay," I answered.

"Keepin' them drunks outa the crapper?" I could hear a juke box or something behind him, and a lot of laughing.

"It's okay, Elmer."

"Just hang in. I'm almost on my way."

A couple of crummy-looking dogs must have heard Elmer and had decided to couple right next to the High Test pump. I ran out and kicked them in the butts, figuring it didn't look so good for the customers, especially when the Cub Scouts came in.

And so the long hot summer went in Elmer's Esso Station, the motorists' haven on US 41, and late at night when Merle Haggard's keening wail battles the heavyside layer and Oral Roberts, sings about that Great Super Service In The Sky, and about changin' plugs on Moses' magic carpet, and that guy comes toolin' in and says: *Gimme fifty cents worth a'reg'lar . . . Check the oil too if you don't mind . . . Put some air in my tires, would ya mister? . . . and wash my windows too, when you get time** . . . my back begins to ache way down low, from all that bending in the grease pit, and I know that Elmer is out

*"Harold's Super Service" (Bobby Wayne), Shade Tree Music Central Songs, BMI.

there somewhere in the American night giving service to those blondes and holding off the Coke man, and keeping those drunks out of the crapper.

7

The Rosetta Stone
of American Culture

"TRAGEDIES OF THE WHITE SLAVES — TAKEN FROM ACTUAL LIFE! FOR GOD SAKE, DO SOMETHING!"

Countless red-necked raw-boned farm boys licked their lips in lustful righteousness as they addressed an envelope, using a chewed, stubby penny pencil, to Johnson Smith & Co., Racine, Wisconsin. They were ordering #1375 from the Big Book or The Catalog. In a few weeks they would have in their horny hands 200 pages of some of the ripest outhouse reading this side of *The Police Gazette.*

Johnson Smith & Co. is and was as totally American as apple pie, far more so in fact, since they do make apple pie most places in the civilized world. Only America could have produced Johnson Smith. There is nothing else in the world like it. Johnson Smith is to Man's darker side what Sears Roebuck represents to the clean-limbed soil-tilling righteous side, a rich compost heap of exploding cigars, celluloid teeth, Anarchist (Stink) Bombs [#6256 "More fun than a Limburger cheese"]. The Johnson Smith catalog is a magnificent smudgy thumbprint of a totally lusty, vibrant, alive, crude Post Frontier society, a society that was, and in some ways still remains, an exotic mixture of moralistic piety and violent primitive humor. It is impossible to find a single dull page, primarily because life in America in the early days of the twentieth century might have been hard, a constant struggle, and almost completely lacking in creature comfort but it certainly was never dull. The simplest activity was, to use a popular phrase of the day, *"fraught with danger."* For example, #R9007, the "Young America" Safety Hammer Revolver, is described as *"very popular with cyclists."* Apparently, to the reader of the day, no explanation was necessary. The mind boggles at the unknown horrors that a "cyclist" daily faced by merely pedalling around the park. The same item is also described as *"excellent for ladies' use."* It is just this sort of thing that makes the Johnson Smith catalog zippier reading than any James Bond fiction. It is hard to believe at this date that the writers of the catalog were dealing with real life of the time. I don't recall ever meeting a "lady" who carried a .32 caliber automatic in her handbag *for immediate use.*

Along the same lines, in the description of #R9022, the Automatic Break-Open Target Revolver (*"it hits the mark!"*), the following sentence occurs: *"You never know when War may come, or you may find yourself dependent upon your skill in shooting for a meal of game."* Such a bald statement would never occur in, say, an Abercrombie & Fitch catalog.

The thing that immediately gets you about the Johnson Smith world is its naked, unashamed realism. It is a world where humor involves the Squirt Ring (#2173): *"an attractive looking diamond that cannot fail to be the center of attraction. The observer experiences a very great surprise";* or the classic Itching Powder: (#6257) *"Thoroughly enjoyable — the intense discomfiture of your victims is highly amusing."* It was the era of the Pig Bladder and W. C. Fields, and subtlety was somehow foreign and feminine.

As history, the Johnson Smith catalog is far more alive than the self-conscious volumes of sociology; #2751–10¢, the *"Boot-*

legger Cigar," says more about the days of Prohibition than anything I've ever read of the period. *"An exact imitation of a real cigar, which consists of a glass tube with a cork in the end. It is really a well-designed flask that can be used to carry any liquid refreshment."* They weren't talking about Orange Crush or Pepsi-Cola. "Bootlegger" is the key word. The image of a man walking around with a glass cigar in his mouth filled with sour mash bourbon is wildly funny and could only be played by W.C. himself.

Another almost extinct phase of the American scene is fully documented by items #7100 through #7176. It is a classic list of emblems of an American phenomenon that flourished in small towns from just after the Civil War through the early 30s; the Lodge, the Brotherhood, the Secret Society. In a day when men had to band together for one reason or another, mainly social, these institutions were really the focal point of life in many a hamlet. Men wore badges proudly and without self-consciousness. For example, #7130 *Panama Canal* stated to the world that the wearer had worked on the famous Canal. This item alone would bring big money in Americana museums today. It sold for twenty-five cents through Johnson Smith. The plumber, the plasterer, the bricklayer, the blacksmith and the carpenter all had badges to be hung proudly from watch-chains (See #7112 through #7116). Are there alive today any men who wore in honor #7167, The Brotherhood of Street-car Trainmen?

For just a quarter a member could get a watch fob proclaiming to everyone that he was in the Sons Of Veterans (#7123). Veterans of what? Probably some war. What war? The Civil War? The Spanish-American War? The War Of The Roses? They never said. Are there any chapters still flourishing? You can see their proud escutcheon in the catalog and probably nowhere else.

Johnson Smith was also the Bible of the go-getting *entrepreneur,* always alert for new opportunities offering "untold riches." "MAKE BIG MONEY STAMPING KEY CHECKS (#7085)" or raising mushrooms in your own Mystery Mushroom Garden which *"has earned several dollars a week for satisfied users."*

Technically, the Johnson Smith catalog is very interesting because it does not represent one period of time. The catalog covers an era that saw *"Civil War watch fobs"* as well as *"Smitty, Dick Tracy and Orphan Annie Wristwatches"* ($3.95, nos. 8050 through 8052), as well as the dawn of the electronic age (#6590: *"this Detector is a radio in itself — 25¢"*).

Every live-wire, life-of-the-party had, in those days, a complete repertory of parlor tricks, totally equipped by Johnson Smith & Co. of Racine, Wisconsin. He was prepared to conquer every social gathering with the sheer audacity of his wit and the subtlety of the prestidigitation he displayed. Apparently it was necessary to bring your equipment to a party in a steamer trunk at least: *Diminishing Billiard Ball* (#3221, 50¢), *The Handkerchief Vanisher, "practically undetectable; never fails"* (#3193), *The Mesmerized Penny: "Defies the law of gravitation"* (#3157) and *The Mysterious King Tut Trick* (#3229, 15¢ Postpaid) were merely basic equipment. The truly dedicated social climber would need the Spirit Medium Ring (#3143) as well as the expensive but effective Mysterious Chalice (#3180, 50¢). This was obviously a time when people provided their own entertainment and did not rely on the movies, TV, or the canned humor of the stand-up comic.

Johnson Smith provided the material for

anyone who wanted to amuse and entertain his friends. Joke books filled several
pages of the catalog and they were highly
functional in a day when people had to
make their own laughs; #1917 *ONE
THOUSAND CHOICE CONUNDRUMS
AND RIDDLES* (10¢) was a smash seller. It
featured such boffolas as:

MAN: Why don't you help me find my
collar button?
FRIEND: I would, but it always gives
me the Creeps!

This crusher must have panicked them
from Kalamazoo to Keokuk, and for only a
dime you got nine hundred and ninety-
nine more, *"enough to last you for years!"*
The truth of the matter is that they were
not exaggerating. Some of those jokes are
still kicking around TV and writers are
earning Big Money selling them to comics
who apparently never read Johnson Smith
& Co.'s catalog. If you think this is mere
philosophizing, it might pay you to read a
couple of these joke books and then watch
TV for a month. This brings up another
significant point about the Johnson Smith
catalog. So much of it is absolutely timeless. For example, the Ouija Board, in-

vented by a Baltimore man as a parlor trick (#6645), is selling in greater numbers today than it did when it was introduced and distributed by Johnson Smith.

The chatty quality of the unknown caption writers is distinct, and seems to emanate from a single, living, crochety yet ribald human being. On the one hand he cozies up to the reader, nudges him in the ribs and says: *"Here's your chance, boys. Put on one of these Bunged-Up Eye disguises. The effect as you enter the room is most bewildering. Real fun!"* (#4355–10¢). On the other hand, he thunders from his soapbox in tones of outraged virtue: *"Your heart will burn and you will wonder how such awful things can be, and you will feel like others that you must become a crusader to go out and fight and tell others and warn against the danger!"* as he exhorts us to buy *FROM DANCE HALL TO WHITE SLAVERY — THE WORLD'S GREATEST TRAGEDY* (#1376, an absolute steal at 35¢).

It is this eerily personal style that sets the tone of this great volume of human desires and vanities. A very necessary yet ubiquitous ingredient of the Johnson Smith catalog is the consistently provocative illustrations, again the work of anonymous,

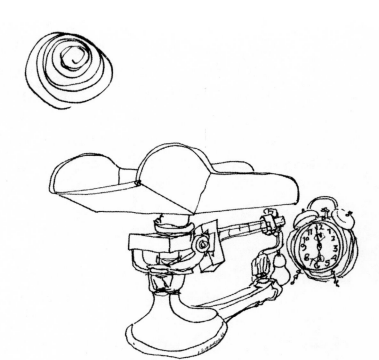

humble artists who probably never signed a picture in their lives. For example, the grotesque drawing illustrating #4353 Joke Teeth With Tongue foreshadowed the best work of the later Surrealists. The man's startled yet strangely evil expression about the eyes as he displays his seven-inch rubber tongue and his gleaming celluloid false teeth is enough to make us wonder what it's all about! His caption writer, obviously inspired by the drawing, rose to extraordinary heights with this item: *"These Joke Teeth And Tongues are just the thing to surprise your friends with. The tongues are extra-long and quite ferocious-looking, and produce the most comical effects. Excellent for Theatrical use."*

Instantly the mind gropes for the dramatic presentation that employs a seven-inch rubber tongue attached to celluloid teeth. It is easy to say, however, that it *would* surprise your friends, at the very least!

On the same page is another fine, unsigned work illustrating *THE ENORMOUS VIBRATING EYE,* obviously the work of an artist of another school. He, nevertheless, perfectly catches the raffish cloddishness of a man who would wear an Enormous Vibrating Eye. The cap he wears in the drawing is a touch of sheer genius. By the way, if you are interested, this is catalog #4356 and sells for 15¢, or $1.35 per dozen if you're a real sport.

Physical infirmities abound in the Johnson Smith humor world. *THE SWOLLEN THUMB* (#2108) is a good example, incidentally illustrated nicely with a pair of rubes looking dolefully at a giant, bulbous thumb.

Apparently another sure-fire laugh-getter was the substitution of phony items for commonplace objects. Most of them were made of soap and were *"guaranteed to liven up any party."* A real wit could spark up his friendly gatherings with soap cheese (*"it might fool even the mice"* — 15¢, #2703) or soap biscuits (*"A few of these mixed in with a dish of regular crackers will really start the fun!"*). You bet, especially after a couple of Martinis!

Soap gumdrops, soap cigars, soap pickles, soap chocolates, and even a bar of soap soap that dyed its user an indelible blue made life exciting to the friends of a Johnson Smith addict. There is no record of the number of murders, assault and battery cases, and simple divorces that this single line of Johnson Smith specialities caused to come about. A man wearing an Enormous Vibrating Eye feeding his wife and kids soap pickles is a commonplace still-life in the world of Johnson Smith.

Everything, or almost everything, came by mail in the early days of the 20th Century. The mailman was often the only link to the great outside world that a largely rural America knew. Mail order catalogs had an enormous appeal to simple folk who rarely saw more than a crossroads general store. During the days just before World War One, few homes were without the Sears Roebuck catalog, the Montgomery Ward catalog, as well as the Johnson Smith & Co. catalog, especially if there were boys in the family. The Johnson Smith catalog was predominately Male in its appeal and was not all fun and games. In fact, the catalog had a kind of Horatio Alger upward-and-onward appeal to the young man of the period. He could order correspondence lessons from Johnson Smith in everything from playing the ukelele to *"NEW AND SIMPLIFIED METHODS OF MIMICRY, WHISTLING AND IMITATIONS"* as well as *"POLISH SELF-TAUGHT"* (#1128, 35¢). In a day when education beyond the Fifth Grade was a rarity, these Self-Help courses were no joke and represented real education to the people who studied by kerosene lamps.

The constant drive for financial success which has played an important role in creating the character of America is well documented throughout the Johnson Smith catalog. Just one example: *THE BOOK OF GREAT SECRETS: ONE THOUSAND WAYS OF GETTING RICH! "To persons who work hard for a living and then don't get it, we have a few plain words to say. Every person wants to make money and wants to make it fast and easy. This book will tell them how."* For only 25¢ this fantastic volume (#1250) outlined money-making schemes ranging all the way from home recipes for Holland Gin to how to make Corn Cures to a formula for treating *"Various diseases to which horses are subject."* I'm curious about the number of people who read this volume and then went on to fame and fortune using the tested formula for making Eye Water or Tomato Catsup that the 25¢ book gave them.

To the superstitious and the basically ignorant, attaining wealth has often seemed to be a matter of luck or secret, sinister, mystic knowledge. Johnson Smith stood ready to provide the struggling clod with the hidden key. If he couldn't make it as an honest veterinarian or plumber he could at least master Hypnotism and gain his ends by treachery. And at a remarkably low cost. Catalog #1559, *MYSTERIES OF CLAIRVOYANCE* is only one example of numerous appeals that Johnson Smith made to the superstitious side of rustic America. *"How to make yourself a perfect operator. This work lifts the curtain and tells what some books only hint at."*

"Discover Thebes and find out where the plunder is hidden."

"To see the issue of all 'Pools' whether in stocks or financial matters. Be the MASTER."

"This book should be kept under lock and key. You don't want everyone to be as wise as yourself!"

All of this for only a thin dime. *"COMPLETE EXPLANATION AND INSTRUCTION OF MESMERISM AND PSYCHOLOGY."* So much for Freud!

The fascinating mixture of primitive mysticism and modern technology is one of the things that make the Johnson Smith catalog so endlessly intriguing. Its pages are jammed full of every human vice and fear. Cupidity, nobility, lust, piety; all are given equal space, and significantly there is no sense of embarrassment or shame anywhere. Violence is taken for granted in almost every form of activity. "Emergencies" are continually encountered on every hand. Johnson Smith was pre-eminent in the field of providing personal tools of mayhem for the righteous. Nowhere is it hinted that the bad guys could just as easily mail in the 25¢ for the *SILENT DEFENDER* or *ALUMINUM GLOVES* (#2095). These case-hardened lightweight knuckledusters are described as *"very useful in an emergency."* The buyer was advised to *"buy one for each hand."*

On the very next page, item #9077, the *SPRING STEEL PATENT TELESCOPIC*

POLICE CLUB is called *"the most reliable arm for self-defense."* It was designed to be telescoped for concealment and could be carried in the hand without being noticed. When an "emergency" arose, this is what happened according to the caption writer: *"Your adversary is caught quite unprepared and is landed a stinging blow of a totally unexpected nature, rendering him completely helpless."* Since this little beauty was made of spring steel, the writer was probably understating the case. The warning *"Do not mistake this club with weak imitations"* (sic) is well taken. Many items displayed in the Johnson Smith catalog carry the same advice. Apparently there were unscrupulous "imitators" everywhere dealing in spurious exploding cigars, sneezing powder, hand grenades and horse liniment. Since Johnson Smith always sold the real thing, there was a sense of security which went with a mailed order to Racine, Wisconsin.

And there was something to it. In the days of glory of the company, mail order flimflams were everywhere. Every magazine was filled with appeals to the unwary. Fifty cents sent off to an important-sounding address in Chicago most often brought nothing in return. Johnson Smith

162

stood like a rock of integrity in the midst of this sneaky landscape. When you ordered a Shimmy Inspector Badge (#2019) you got precisely that: shiny, 2½" by 6½", it made *"a big hit"* with your friends. It was ten cents well spent.

Johnson Smith also recognized something that has only recently begun to appear in more sophisticated Advertising circles. They were well ahead of their time in many ways. They realized that advertising must be entertaining in itself, whether or not the customer buys. They knew that if he read the catalog for sheer enjoyment eventually something would grab him. Throughout the catalog, usually at the bottom of the page, little gratis knee-slappers are thrown in.

LAWYER: You say your wife attacked you with a death-dealing weapon. What was it?
LITTLE TOD: A fly swatter.

As feeble as this joke was, it made no attempt to sell. It was just there. There are dozens sprinkled throughout the catalog like raisins in rice pudding.

There was one thing more than any other in the entire catalog that was identified with the company. They were sent everywhere and probably were as close to being a classic in the field of vulgarity as any other single practical joke ever created. Johnson Smith introduced this zinger to the waiting populace, who immediately embraced it wherever yahoos proliferated and low buffoonery flourished. In fact, it sets the tone of the entire Johnson Smith catalog which you are about to enjoy and no doubt cherish, as your immediate ancestors did.

I commend you to #2953, which sold for a trivial twenty-five cents. The first time it appeared in the catalog few suspected that it would attain such timeless significance. Even today one hears references to its unfailing success at achieving hilarity and bringing cringing embarrassment to its victims. There are few alive who have not heard of it, yet most have never actually seen one. Johnson Smith & Co. of Racine, Wisconsin, still carries a full line and if you'd care to order one they would be delighted to comply.

THE WHOOPEE CUSHION says it all. Here is what Johnson Smith has to say about their classic: *"The Whoopee Cushion or Poo-Poo Cushion as it is sometimes called is made of rubber. It is inflated in much the same manner as an ordinary rubber balloon and then placed on a chair. When the victim unsuspectingly sits upon the cushion, it gives forth noises that can be better imagined than described."* The accompanying illustration leaves nothing to the imagination.

This catalog today is just a very funny coffee-table curiosity, because we are still too close to the life and times it describes. In two hundred years it will be a truly significant historical and social document. It could even be the Rosetta Stone of American culture. Students of the future, deciphering it, will know far more about us through its pages than through any other single document I know of. Read it, enjoy it, and honor it. It is about us.

8

One Day the Fog Lifted —

Juneau is one of the most beautiful, exciting, curious places on earth. It lies at the base of a ring of the most perpendicular mountains I have ever seen. They rise straight up a couple of hundred yards from the main street, and just keep going on up and up, and way up there in the low clouds that hang over Juneau are mountain goat, roaring waterfalls, and very large, broad-shouldered bears.

The 13,000 or so Juneauians are unevenly divided between those who spend most of the night going in and out of the Red Dog Saloon and those few who denounce them. After the Red Dog, and Ty Tyson, the bartender, begin to taper off around 1:30 a.m., the Dreamland opens for business and roars until the last bear staggers home bleary-eyed.

From the minute my Alaskan Airlines 737 flipped over into a nearly perpendicular bank and whipped through the scudding clouds, whistling along the sheer face of a cliff for, of necessity, one of the hairiest air approaches anywhere, I knew that Juneau, and Alaska, was totally, completely and thoroughly real. A story, surely apocryphal, which Alaska Airlines pilots love to tell over their intercom as you approach Juneau Airport, is that Pan Am flew in and out of there for years, and then one day the fog lifted, the pilots saw the mountains and immediately went on strike for hazard pay.

I've seen a lot of stuff about Alaska. I've seen films, and endless color slides, but all of it and none of it came anywhere near catching what it's really like. After a few hours in Juneau I knew damn well that it would take dispatches from a lot more than one city to give you any idea of this fantastic state. For one thing, Juneau is very different from the other parts of Alaska that I visited. The Japanese current lies just offshore, giving Juneau a climate that in some ways resembles Seattle or Portland. But that is only statistically. There is rarely a day when it doesn't rain in Juneau, and perpetually low, twisting clouds drift over and around the mountains, reaching down the gullies like some eerie grey smoke. This makes Juneau feel sort of enclosed, intimate and turned in on itself. The old cliche "If you don't like the weather, wait five minutes; it'll change" is absolutely true in Juneau. It is not a cliche but an accurate description of Juneauian weather. The inlet that splits Juneau lies deep in a valley and up and down, almost continually, float planes drone just under the cloud level a few hundred feet over the icy water. The float plane is to Alaska what the family car is to anywhere else. A large percentage of the population is licensed to fly, and everywhere are red and white, hairy-looking Stinsons and Cessnas scarred and tested by years of bush flying.

People in Alaska don't own cars; they own vehicles. They are very unsentimental or romantic about automobiles. They are used purely as machinery, the only criterion being, apparently, "does it work?" If it doesn't, forget it. The cars are almost all battered, and have that hell-with-it-all look that everything else in Alaska, including the people, seems to have. Not many foreign cars seem to make it in Juneau, and I would guess mostly due to the parts problem as well as the insane grades and the gravel roads which are really tough on transmissions and differentials. You see a lot of International Harvester Scouts, some Rovers, a few Jeepsters, and a lot of plain, ordinary battered Fords and Chevys. The

Volkswagen, of course, is on hand, and I'm beginning to suspect that when the world turns cold and Man departs, the only thing left will be VWs and cockroaches. Maybe they are the meek. Who knows. A few Volvos can be seen as well as a very occasional Saab, but for the most part any foreign cars around are usually driven by tourists who have come up the Alaskan Highway from the West Coast.

By the way, no Alaskan ever calls it the Alcan Highway. That went out with the Andrews Sisters and "Johnny Got A Zero." It *is* the Alaskan Highway and don't you forget it. No matter what you call it, though, it is a rough stretch of roadway and can be as treacherous in many ways as any stretch of highway in the world. It is also wildly exciting and beautiful. If you want to take a couple of weeks off and do something that you will never forget, that trip up the Alaskan Highway will do until they run excursion capsules to the Moon.

There is one thing about Juneau that completely floored me, something that in my wildest imagination I would never have guessed, and dammit, it pains me to report this, but here it is. Would you believe that one of the really big pains in the neck in Juneau is *parking!* And I mean it's really a

169

hassle. If you think you've got it bad wherever the hell you are, you have seen nothing until you try to get a slot in Juneau. Good God Almighty! They have been known to fight it out on the street with .44 Magnums over a parking place. It's hard to figure out why this is, until you look closely at the town and realize that in spite of all the wilderness that surrounds Juneau, the actual town itself is jammed into a little space among the towering cliffs and there is damn little room on those narrow, twisting streets for hulking Toronados and billowing Electras. Most of the streets are only two cars wide, so spaces are actually rented by the month and they don't come cheap. The prices in Juneau for practically everything are staggering by Lower 48 standards. (By the way, Alaskans generally refer to us as living in the "Lower 48" or the "South," or occasionally "The Lesser States.") A guy stuffing junk mail into envelopes can earn $600 a month in Juneau, so naturally prices are incredible by conventional standards. Almost everything has to be flown in or trucked up the Alaskan highway, so a $3.00 hamburger is common. A breakfast of a couple of eggs, french fries, coffee and toast will go anywhere from $2.50 to three and a half, with everything else on the same scale. A fairly modest steak will go maybe $9.00, so when you head North be sure to bring plenty of cabbage unless you intend to live off what you can catch or shoot. Gas is about 70¢ a gallon. Oddly enough, you get used to the prices very quickly and after a while you don't think anything of 40¢ Coke machines and 20¢ candy bars.

I checked into the Baranof Hotel, named after a Russian who ran the show in the Juneau area back in the days before Seward had committed his Folly and bought the whole state — mountains, glaciers, polar bears and all for 2¢ an acre. I stepped out on the street ten minutes later, turned left and headed for the Red Dog, which features an enigmatic Indian sporting a haircut in the Napoleonic style singing show tunes, accompanied by an even more Buddha-like Indian lady on the piano. The Red Dog is the kind of place "colorful" bars in the Lower 48 try to imitate, but never quite pull off. Five minutes later I was aware that I was in the presence of Big League drinkers. As one Alaskan put it to me: "What the hell else can you do? There's only two things to do in Alaska, and drinking is one of them." They stagger

171

172

in and out of the swinging doors with purpose and dedication. These are not casual grab-a-Martini-on-the-way-home-from-work types; they are *drinkers* and everywhere I went in Alaska it was the same. It is a state where women are women and men are after them, and if you have any doubts about your Sexual status they will be quickly resolved in the land where men toil for gold and the Northern lights play o'er the skies like the chariots of Hell.

I wanted to go fishing, and I ran into Steve Hildebrand, a 16-year-old Alaskan and the son of the Acting City Manager of Juneau. His sardonic wit drives his Old Man right up the wall, and is typical of Alaskans. A gentle cool rain, of course, was falling when I wheeled my rented, shuddering Ford Galaxie up the narrow gravel road to Steve's house, which sits on a high bluff overlooking the whole city with a view of unparalleled magnificence. He came trotting out with a couple of beat-up spinning rods and a canvas fish bag, which he tossed into the back seat. He then threw on the front seat between us as evil-looking a US Army standard issue .45 calibre automatic as I had ever seen. Also two full clips of copper-nosed slugs. "Jesus Keerist," I thought, "what kind of a cuckoo am I stuck with?"

I tried to play it cool. "Ah . . . what's the roscoe for?"

"The what?" Steve mumbled as he pulled his bright yellow elf hat down over his ears.

"The forty-five. The cannon, you dope. What the hell's it for?"

He wiped the sweat off the inside of the windshield with a dripping rag.

"Bears," he said, as matter-of-factly as you would say "cheeseburger" or "Johnny Carson."

"It won't stop 'em, but it might scare 'em." Naturally, being a totally hip City type I thought I was being put on. It wasn't until later that night that I found I wasn't, and that Steve did not kid.

We drove out to Fish Creek, a magnificent tumbling stream, crystal clear and ice-cold that wound between towering hills and through great forest. Using a red and white spoon, within ten minutes I had savage strikes which broke the line twice, losing lure and all, and finally hooked a salmon that fought for a good fifteen minutes before I beached him. He went about eight pounds, not large by local standards, but great eating later that night when the hotel baked him for me. I landed another at least twice that size and released him. By that time the mosquitoes were really getting mean and the rain was coming down harder. Even the magnificent bald eagle which had been circling above us, watching us suspiciously, his talons at the ready, decided to pack it in for the night. So we decided to take the hint and drove back to town. The fishing in Alaska is incredible!

On the way back, Steve and I talked cars. He is a fanatic Grand Prix nut, but like most other aficionados in Alaska is starved for information. Car magazines are almost impossible to get. The demand far exceeds the supply. The only information they get is from Jeff Scott's network radio shows, and that's about it.

"Hey Steve, I hereby officially propose the creation of the Grand Prix d'Juneau," I barked in my best Robert Service manner as we scudded past a float plane base in the drifting rain. He laughed bitterly.

"Yeah, I can just see it now. Jackie Stewart roaring up the Perseverance Trail, a two thousand foot sheer drop six inches from his spinning wheels. To his left, the sharp-rising precipice of Mount Juneau, and in the undergrowth ten-foot bears waiting to play ping-pong with his Formula One mount. Three seconds behind him, his nemesis Graham Hill making up

175

lost time after a nasty mauling by a female bear and her three fun-loving cubs at the Mendenhall River S-turn, his teeth clenched with determination. . . ."

"Stop! I can't stand it." Steve rocked with laughter as the torrents of rain roared down our windshield, the wipers hardly making a dent in the downpour.

"That would sure be some race," he said, "the Grand Prix d'Juneau. Oh boy! It would be the greatest race in the world. . . ."

He trailed off with a note of hopelessness in his voice. Both of us said nothing as we drove back to his house, with the Colt .45 between us and the dead salmon on the back seat. It *would* be the greatest race in the world, the most spectacular, the most grueling and without a doubt the most beautiful. Yep, I hereby officially propose the Grand Prix d'Juneau, to stand alongside Monaco and Le Mans: a supreme test of car, driver, and bear.

Later that night Steve's mother bawled him out for taking the .45 along on a fishing trip.

"If I hear of you taking that .45 out to Fish Creek again you're really going to be in trouble. Don't ever let me hear of you going out again with less than a 30-06.

176

That .45 is nothing. You hear me?"

Steve sulked. I gulped.

"You know what happened to Jimmy," she said.

"Yeah," was all Steve answered. I decided I didn't want to know what had happened to Jimmy. Alaska is that kind of country.

9

Fun City

There is no question about it. Good old mankind, an exotic branch of the animal world of which I am indubitably a part, is one of the most adaptable organisms known to science. He ranges freely from the fetid jungles at the equator to the very poles, perpetually icebound and forbidding to all but the most hardy of species. He even manages to knock out a few golf balls on the Moon. Let hooded cobras or flying squirrels try that one.

He also — and this is one of the major differences that exist between the lesser primates and the notorious Upright Ape That Thinks — creates, often, his own environment, both good and bad. There is some suspicion in certain theological quarters that for centuries we have misinterpreted a key passage in the Scriptures, the one that goes: "And the Meek shall inherit the earth." It is now felt that the Meek referred to were not the Walter Mittys or the Peace advocates, or even Ralph Nader, but instead the lowly cockroaches. Lowly? It all depends on how you interpret "lowly." Like man, the cockroach makes it damn near everywhere he goes, and more than that, makes it big. He has been found in deserted trappers' cabins at 70° below zero, living off, apparently, icicles and polar bear dung, and proliferating at that. Anyone who has spent any time in the tropics knows how well he does there. A lone cockroach was discovered aboard one of the Apollo capsules on a flight to the Moon. He disappeared shortly after discovery, and there is suspicion that now, for the first time, there *is* life on the Moon.

The chief difference between mankind and the cockroach is that the one continually bitches over his fate while the other stoically plods on, uncomplaining, with never a glance backward nor a sigh for what might have been.

Thoughts like this are the kind that come easily to me as I struggle my way uptown through the heavy miasma of hydrocarbons and obscenities that hangs thickly like a shifting yellow curtain of doom over Sixth Avenue in Fun City. For those of you who are not familiar with this classic urban thoroughfare — known officially as The Avenue Of The Americas; better known to more literate cab drivers as The Armpit Of Manhattan — it runs due North, theoretically one-way, from somewhere south of Greenwich Village right up the gut of Manhattan, past such cultural centers as Macy's and Gimbel's, encompassing the Porny belt around 42nd Street, and then finally ending in an ungodly traffic snarl at the south end of Central Park.

Driving in midtown New York is a specialty as highly difficult and rarified as, say, lion taming or Japanese Sumo wrestling. It requires a high degree of pugnacity, total selfishness and a complete careless disregard for what is called in other quarters and more civilized sections of our country, the Rights Of Others. The true Manhattan driver never concedes that the "others" deserve any rights whatsoever, and in fact he rarely admits that there *are* "others." He combines incredible, almost inhuman qualities of stoicism with the ferocity usually associated with the male rhinoceros in rutting season.

For you fortunates who live out there in the Great Outside beyond the Hudson, who believe that magnificent driving is what you see under the auspices of NASCAR or at Indy, I can only say that a mid-day session with a Manhattan hackie through the garment district is well worth the exorbitant price, if for sheer instructionary and thrill content alone. I have studied the breed for years, and a considerable portion of my life's fortune has been spent keeping their rapacious meters ticking over merrily, each tick moving me closer and closer to the Poor House while often taking me away from my destination.

Manhattan cabs are born old. As you struggle into the back seat at, say 8th Street and 6th Avenue, of the yawing, sagging, stinking hulk which has lurched curbward in your direction, its glaring toadlike pilot hunched over his greasy steering wheel, a seven-cent cigar clamped in his teeth, you are startled to find that the cab itself often has less than 3,000 miles on the speedometer. Four days out of the showroom and already a grizzled veteran of combat. Crashing from pothole to pothole, knee-deep in a rich compost of cigarette butts, candy wrappers and drying urine, you hurtle northward toward your lunch date. Around you are thousands of other yellow, barnacle-encrusted wrecks, each driver being a total professional. In all my years of New York cab riding I have yet to find the colorful, philosophical cabdriver that keeps popping up on the late movies. There are no William Bendixes or Lloyd Nolans or Jimmy Cagneys pushing hacks in the big town. If there are, I sure as hell haven't found them.

The nature of the car in the big city itself is something that requires a little explanation. Month after month magnificent, gleaming color ads leap out at you from the pages of *Car and Driver.* To a New Yorker these fantasy images of sparkling sculptured masterpieces are as remote from our daily lives as, say, Oz or Samarkand. It is common for a man to take possession of a new, sleek Firebird on Tuesday and by late Thursday afternoon it has been pounded and battered into a Fiat 850. By the following Wednesday he is driving an ancient Morgan three-wheeler and then, magically, maybe mercifully, the roving mobs of car snatchers have relieved him of what's left and he's back to hailing cabs.

A daily sight along the expressways is the superb team precision of the vultures who can be seen hourly stripping anything that slows down under 10 mph, from a Mark XI heavy tank to a Honda 305. There is some talk in local circles that Car Stripping will eventually become an Olympic team event, at last giving the underprivileged the chance to show their true skills on TV, with Keith Jackson doing the commentary, produced by Roone Arledge for the "Wide Wide World of Sports." It has been said, although perhaps apocryphally, that there are certain operators in Brooklyn who can remove a full set of mag wheels from a Corvette proceeding on the Long Island Expressway at 60 mph, or the legal limit, with the driver totally unaware of his loss until he hits Hempstead where the potholes start to peter out. Naturally, this gives rise to a certain jumpiness among us irrational dreamers who persist in attempting to own a car in New York.

Garage space alone is a can of worms that's beyond the comprehension of anyone who has never really lived in Manhattan. It is not uncommon for a car owner to shell out more for a tiny slot of dirty, greasy, rat-infested space grudgingly allotted him by snarling, rapacious thugs than he does for his apartment housing his beloved and his two precious goldfish. He must contact his "garage," actually a sagging red-brick 200-year-old firetrap manned by venomous dacoits, fully ten days or more before he wishes to use his battered vehicle.

184

Contacted at last by telephone they answer with a surly grunt, that is if the local AT&T mob, which currently seems to be in the hands of Doctor No bent on world destruction for his own mad design, allows him to get through at all, after taking upwards of ten gratuitous dimes from the sufferer. The exchange of pleasantries goes roughly like this:

"YEH?" (accompanied by heavy breathing and a brief period of phlegmy hawking and the sound of copious spitting, probably on someone's Aston Martin).

"Uh . . . excuse me, but I'd like to have my car, sir, if . . ."

"FER CRISSAKE, we're BUSY! What the Hell!" (The sound of muffled crashings drowns out conversation momentarily.)

"I have that blue Fiat, the one . . ."

"Fer Crissake that Fiat's inna damn BASEMENT! Whaddaya expect me to do, godammit, it's Tuesday!!"

"I know, I'm sorry, sir, but there's nothing I can do about it. I got a call that my mother had a stroke and I have to . . ."

(The beseecher is interrupted at this point by unintelligible shouting in the phone. A fight has broken out at the garage. Apparently another car owner has arrived unexpectedly, demanding his machine.

Naturally, immediate disciplinary action is being taken by the "attendants," who must maintain the upper hand else mob rule would take over. Amid the hullabaloo he hears the familiar voice of his telephone friend.)

"HEY HEINIE, THAT FAT NUT WIT' DA FIAT WANTS HIS TIN CAN. WHEN CANYA GIVE IT TA HIM?" (There is a burst of offstage laughter accompanied by a smattering of obscenity too ripe for family reading.)

"When d'y wannit?"

"Well, I thought . . ."

"We can't get it outa the basement before Friday. Crissake, you guys call up an' want yer car widout no notice or nothin!"

"I'm sorry, sir. I'll be over Friday, sir, I hate to bother you, but . . ."

(He is drowned out by maniacal squealing of brakes followed by a muffled thud and a tinkling of glass. The line goes dead.)

Chances are 30–1 that when the victim arrives at the garage the following Friday no one on the premises will remember his call or even his face, since he has only been in the clutches of the mob for three years and can't expect recognition, and will be told to come back next Wednesday at the earliest. For this he antes up $90 a month and is expected never to mention the bashed-in doors, the flattened trunk, the smashed grille or the beer cans he finds in the front seat and the unmistakable evidence that at least three people and a dog have been camping out in his pride and joy while running down the battery listening to the Mets and striking kitchen matches on his knurled walnut instrument panel.

Everywhere else in the country, cars have distinct differences. Some are Jaguars; others are Pintos. There are Gremlins and Corvettes. They even have distinctive colors. There are blues, greens, Cardinal reds, and even eggshell whites. To a New Yorker this seems almost something out of the halcyon past, the days of simple pleasures like home-made bread and Fourth of July fireworks. By the third day of its life in New York City all these characteristics of the automobile have all but disappeared. The Jersey crud which drifts down inexorably from what used to be the Heavens, bearing its deadly load of rare and subtle acids, its exotic poisons and mysterious gases, has obliterated all signs of distinctive coloration. The car becomes a curious mouldy dun color, which is distinctively Manhattan in character as it resembles the mole-like inhabitants' complexions.

Repeated bashings, side-swipings, ding-ing and general hammerings have formed the machine into its basic non-identifiable lumpish form. The job is completed by the locust swarm of humanoid car levellers who systematically denude every vehicle of its hubcaps, nameplates, badges, antennas and whatever else might have made it vaguely distinctive from its fellows. It is now an urban car; tough, tenacious, and totally anonymous, a fitting companion for the New Yorker himself.

Only the cabdriver, like the ancient sea-faring man, commands the rolling seas of New York traffic. He has his own battle code and like most soldiers has a vast dis-dain for the civilian. Mayors come and mayors go; traffic engineers rise and fall. The New York hackie hates them all. It is a matter of record that *no* licensed New York cabdriver has uttered so much as a mildly civil remark about an incumbent mayor since the late unlamented James Walker, better known as Jimmy The Slick to his bootlegger friends, passed out in a Checker on 49th Street and upon awak-ening tipped the driver with a $20 bill. Legend has it that the hackie, in a clear voice, stated, "Now dere's a good Mayor," although this is in dispute.

The cabdrivers' attitude toward civilian drivers goes like this: You've been seated in a cab with meter ticking away steadily for nineteen minutes at the corner of 33rd Street and Sixth Avenue in a gigantic tangle of unmoving machines.

CABBIE: (red neck glowing) "Y'know what they could do to clean up this whole mess? I'll tell ya what they could do if Lindsay wasn't such a crummy crook. I'll tell ya what they could do."

PASSENGER: (rising to the bait) "What could they do?" (clouds of carbon monoxide swirling around his head and gradually dissolving his new wash-and-wear suit)

CABBIE: "Ya know what they could do? I'll tell ya what they could do if that Lindsay wasn't such a crummy crook. Boy, them stupes what voted for him got what they deserved, an' now the crummy crook wants ta be President!"

PASSENGER: "What could they do?"

CABBIE: "What could they do about what?" (He glances suspiciously into the rear view mirror.)

PASSENGER: (his eyes beginning to pop slightly due to the fact that the temperature in the sagging Plymouth has risen to the near-200° mark) "You were telling me what they could do about the traffic."

(Ahead, the driver of a giant tractor-trailer rig plastered with ancient VOTE FOR GOLDWATER *stickers has commenced a listless fistfight with an unidentified male Caucasian, medium build.)*

CABBIE: "Oh yeah, well if they wasn't so stupid they would ban alla civilian cars from d'roads. Kick 'em off. That's what's causin' alla traffic jams. If that pansy Lindsay wasn't such a stupid crook!"

(The Passenger, glancing around at the vast tangled traffic jam, noticing that there is not a single civilian car in sight, nothing but a sea of yellow cabs and red-necked drivers, all demanding the immediate banishment of non-cabs from the road, settles into moody silence, attempting to while away the ticking-off metered hours by scrounging amid the rubble heap on the cab floor, looking for something to

190

read. Noticing a furtive movement under an encrusted pile of cigar butts and bottle caps he suspects there might be some sort of lizard or maybe a rat sharing his ride. He gives up scrounging and sits patiently awaiting the time when the traffic moves again. He has been here before. Unlike J. Alfred Prufrock, his life is not measured out in coffee spoons but flag-drops and meter ticks. The little white numbers in the grimy glass window mount higher and higher as he squats amid the rubble, sharing with the cockroach the rare ability to adapt to totally alien environments, his lungs operating rhythmically in shallow gasps, extracting what tiny nourishment there is from the putrid atmosphere of his adopted environment. He awakens from his torpor momentarily to continue his listless conversation with the pilot ahead.)

PASSENGER: "How come you got two plastic Christs on the dashboard?"

CABBIE: (relighting the stub of his cigar — which has gone out due to lack of oxygen) "The one onna left belongs to the night man."

It's no wonder that the beautiful magazine ads extolling the glories of Fun City read like fantasy fiction to the average New Yorker.

10

S.P.L.A.T.!

"And so concludes Part Three of NBC's five part salute to Pollution, an in-depth study of Environmental pollution starring Glen Campbell, Frank Sinatra, The Supremes, The Smothers Brothers, and MC'd by Red Skelton. Next week . . ."

I snapped off the set and yawned as a thought crossed my mind. My god, it sure gets you tired trying to keep up with each major crisis. I remembered the good old days of Ban The Bomb with a faint tinge of mauve nostalgia. Ah, the simple problems of yore. I wonder what the Ban The Bombers are doing now? Probably raising kids and fighting crabgrass. Oh well.

The current major crisis, the Environment, carried along with it the same old inevitable crowd of "experts" who predict, predictably, the imminent end of Mankind. For as long as I remember, some authority or another has stated irrevocably that the end was in sight. A few more years and it would all be over. Oh well.

I poured myself a little unpolluted bourbon and sipped thoughtfully. I wonder what happened to that guy at Harvard or some place who maintained stoutly that the astronauts would bring back deadly unknown bacilli from the Moon. Jesus, that one sure petered out. And then the gang of concerned experts who used to sit around on TV panels on Sunday afternoons, jabbering about bomb shelters. Now there was a great crew of doomsayers.

I flipped on the stereo and idly rifled the smudgy pages of *Copulation*, an underground journal of the sexual revolution edited by a defrocked Benedictine monk. Like all underground papers it was available at every news stand. My attention was caught briefly by an article describing the moving intellectual experiences of a seventeen year old female heroin addict at an orgy on 9th Street which somehow involved, among other creatures, a gelded chimpanzee. My mind just wasn't on it. Maybe it was the turgid prose. I glanced over the Want Ads, noting that sado-masochist Lonely Hearts clubs had apparently become one of the major industries of Manhattan, along with underground homosexual film festivals.

I flung the miserable rag aside. If a paper

could have acne, that one had it. I was restless. It was one of those milky Sunday afternoons that you get from time to time in New York in August: temperature in the 90s, heat rising in shimmering waves from the tops of dented, filthy yellow cabs. I usually try to get out of town on a weekend like this, but I had missed connections. Here I was, alone, pacing my apartment like Captain Ahab stumping around the quarter-deck of the *Pequod.*

I tossed off another bourbon, which seemed to instantly produce an overwhelming sleepiness. My air conditioner was out, so the room was hot and muggy. I struggled with a window trying to get a little air. A breath of New York atmosphere oozed in.

I sniffed. A familiar New York aroma filled my lungs, made dank by too much city living. God, how I hated that smell! Every summer it rose from the lush neighborhoods of New York's East Side like a great cloud of swamp gas from the Dismal Swamp. It somehow was the other side of the coin of the lives of the Beautiful People. My breath came in shallow gasps as I tottered over to my zebra skin Castro convertible. I flung myself headlong among the ravaged pile of old *New Yorker*s and

196

soon my fevered soul drifted off to sleep, greased on its way by Jack Daniel's.

A few brief, fitful dreams of a chaotic nature and suddenly, without warning, I found myself in a sea of bright lights; cameras with blinking red eyes peered at me; Steve Allen, looking deeply concerned, was asking me a question. He was flanked by David Susskind, and Malcolm Boyd, the Showbiz priest.

"You say you represent S.P.L.A.T.? An organization devoted to combatting environmental pollution?" Allen's brow furrowed as he turned on his best Involved Citizen look.

"That is correct," I found myself saying.

"Well, Mr. Shepherd, and just what does S.P.L.A.T. stand for?" David Susskind asked this one, his fingertips pressing together making a tiny pyramid. He nodded knowingly in his best Liberal manner. Malcolm Boyd waved at the camera and pointed to the dust jacket of another book he had just written.

"I'd rather not say, if you don't mind," I answered, conscious of a murmur out in the darkness where the great studio audience had assembled.

"Come now, it must stand for something? After all, you have over twelve million members."

"It certainly does," I replied, my confidence rising as I noticed that Susskind had a bit of dried chicken soup on his lapel.

"It's not that I want to hide anything, you understand. It's just that there are probably women and children watching today."

"Yes, Jesus said to me the other day, when we were out jogging together, 'Blessed are the little children.' " Malcolm Boyd was off and running with the Lord again. "In fact, I just cut an LP on this very subject. It's called . . ."

Allen raised his hand casually. "Easy, Malc. We'll plug the record at the end of the show." Boyd frantically held up the record jacket and looked disappointed that the camera had winked out and was now pointing at Susskind.

"It's in Stereo!" he squeaked.

"We don't expect to come up with all the answers today. After all, the Environmental Pollution crisis is very complex, but we Concerned people feel that the Liberal Establishment particularly, relating itself to the suppressed minorities, the first victims of smog, recognize that the certain amount of sacrifice and painful re-evaluation plus

199

cooperation among the more favored elements of the Society . . ."

Susskind had the bit in his teeth and in his inimitable fashion was charging off into the wild blue yonder, spraying cliches recklessly in all directions. I found myself nodding as he droned on.

Luckily a commercial cut him off in mid-platitude. The commercial seemed to be about a lady who found blue water in her john, and a three-inch tall man in a rubber rowboat as well.

"C'mon, Shepherd, what do you mean you can't tell us what S.P.L.A.T. stands for? This is an Adult panel. After all, it's Sunday afternoon, when the Serious shows are on. You can come right out and say it on this show, right boys?"

Susskind nodded gravely. Malcolm Boyd said, "I'll buy that."

"Well, it has to do with Pollution, all right, I can tell you that. We're really getting Militant to boot. You bet!"

"I presume your organization . . ." Susskind crinkled his brow thoughtfully ". . . deals with problems of an Environmental nature."

"You bet!" I interrupted. "And how!"

"One that concerns all the peoples?" Susskind had used one of his favorite words. He's at his best when dealing with Peoples.

"Everybody I know!"

"Folks . . ." Allen beamed at the studio audience out in the darkness. "Shepherd here can come right out and say it, can't he? We're all grownups here."

The audience applauded, with a few whistles and foot stamps thrown in.

"You see, like I said, they're grown up. Well, how about it? What does SPLAT stand for?"

"Don't blame me if you get outraged letters." I fenced for time.

"Our unseen television audience is mature." Allen smiled benignly at me.

"Well, okay. It stands for Society for the Prevention and Limitation of Animal Turds."

A great roar of applause. More whistles and catcalls from the audience. I thought I detected a few screams.

"Eh? What was that?" Susskind, who was not in the habit of listening, appeared confused.

"Society for the Prevention and Limitation of Animal Turds," I repeated.

Susskind disappeared briefly under the desk.

"The other day I had a talk with the

201

Lord on that very subject. The humble creatures of the field are blessed unto . . ."

"Hold it, Boyd." Allen silenced him.

"Let's get this straight, Shepherd. Are you anti-animal? If so . . ."

"No! Heavens no!" I broke in. "It's just that here in New York every summer you're knee-deep in. . . ."

"Easy Shepherd! This is television!" Allen glowered sternly at me.

"What my Aunt Emily called Doggie Dirties, and I can tell you . . ."

Susskind, who seemed to have recovered, waded in:

"Our poor dumb brethren, an oppressed minority which under this sick system should at least be given the vote, and . . ."

"Militant? You say your group is getting militant, eh?" Allen had alertly picked up a key word that is necessary in any intellectual discussion of our day.

"Yes, *militant*. That is correct." I ran my hand through the Afro wig I had recently purchased at a shop in the Village, using my American Express credit card.

"We sure are getting militant. No telling where it will lead."

"How do you mean Militant?" Boyd chimed in, his face wreathed in a beatific smile. "Ah, it is blessed to forgive and

202

those who wield the mighty sword . . ."

"Cut it out, Boyd. Save that for your show at the Bitter End tonight. We only got a half an hour."

Allen, a firm handed emcee, guided the show steadfastly.

"I say when a system of popular democracy, based on mutual trust, fails the little peoples, militancy is the inevitable . . ." Susskind, like Old Man River, rolled on, his words rich, sonorous, with the singsong beat of phrases used over and over.

"Save it for your own show, Dave." Allen nodded in my direction, indicating that I should go on.

"We tried reason; even the courts. All that's left now is Confrontation!" I peered at the panel through my jet black shades. They quailed before me, recognizing as all good Liberals do, that militant confrontation is the hallmark of the Righteous.

"Just what form does your militancy take?" Allen asked, leaning forward over his microphone.

"Well, we picket the ASPCA, for one."

"Why?" Susskind gasped in humane horror.

"Well, we're *for* cruelty to animals. They're plenty cruel to us. It's time the worm turned!"

203

"I am deeply shocked. As a reasonable citizen of good will, I must say, and I wish to make this clear, that I can scarcely believe that in this enlightened age anyone could be as depraved . . ." Susskind wrung his hands as he spoke, great tears rolling down his cheeks. He sobbed in conclusion.

"Yes," I went on, "we're tired of having puppy poo-poo, as our lady members call it, all over our sandals, not to mention our bare feet. We got a slogan: Kick A Squatting Dog In The Ass Today. You probably saw our buttons."

"Say, I like that." Allen led the audience in a brief cheer. "It would make a nice song title." He turned to his piano and sang in a quavery voice:

"Kick a squatting dog in the aaaas today
Yeah yeah yeah
Boot him in the rump, I saaaay
Yeah, baby!
You and I together . . .
Yeah, yeah, yeah . . ."

Allen hunched over the piano, caught up in the surge of creativity. Susskind dabbed at his eyes with a handkerchief that bore the embroidered insignia of the ACLU. Boyd crossed himself briefly and held up his LP to let the audience know where *he* stood on Good and Evil.

"We also," I plunged ahead doggedly amid the hubbub, "organized nose-rubbing Action Squads."

Allen stopped dead in mid-note. Boyd flushed slightly and appeared to be fingering a crucifix. Susskind nodded his patriarchal grey head in disbelief, indicating sorrow at the depravity to which Man can fall.

"Yesireebob, that's one of our most effective counter measures!"

"You mean . . ." Susskind was in full cry again, "you mean those poor, innocent oppressed little doggies are attacked by your Fascist thugs — and I feel justified in calling them that — are so outraged and set upon by the sick Establishment which you represent as to have their sensitive little noses come into contact with . . . ?"

He blew his sensitive nose emotionally into his ACLU handkerchief.

"Now wait a minute, Dave. You don't mind if I call you Dave? After all, this is television. You got it all wrong." I hitched up my dashiki, which was itching me between the shoulderblades.

"Well, I should hope so!" Malcolm Boyd, his brow furrowed with concern,

205

took the stand. "To turn the other cheek, and to coin a phrase, to suffer doggie doo-doo is the Christian way to forgive, and . . ."

Allen cut in sharply at this point, his eye on the studio clock. "Explain yourself, Shepherd." He was not smiling.

"You see, we rub *owners'* noses in the doggie doo-doo, every time we catch an Airedale or a Beagle letting it go in the middle of a sidewalk. We grab the owner by the neck and . . ."

"Watch it, Shepherd!" Allen's tone had become menacing.

"You oughta hear 'em holler. The other day the Squad gave the treatment to a couple of fags that had these nine Afghans on a leash, and you never heard such shrieking and whooping in your life! They learned a lesson they won't forget soon. Then there was this old lady with a bulldog . . ."

"That certainly answers our questions about militancy. Now let's move on into other areas." Allen was back to smiling again.

"It's getting to the point where a new breed of connoisseurs has developed that . . ."

"Connoisseurs?" Allen seemed relieved

206

to be on a safe subject. "Connoisseurs? You mean, art connoisseurs?"

I answered: "A true Manhattanite, by the merest whiff, can tell you whether the little bundle of joy was left by a Pekinese, a Dalmatian, a Great Dane or an Airedale."

"Oh come on." Susskind wore his skeptical face. "Surely you're not telling us of Liberal persuasion that. . . ."

"Not to mention Yorkies, Dachshunds, Labrador Retrievers, Bull Terriers and Springer Spaniels."

"You mean . . . ?" Allen sounded interested. "Just by the aroma you can . . . ?"

"Yes, right! St. Bernards, Chows, Rat Terriers, Blue Tick Hounds; the whole smelly lot. It's a new hobby. You might as well make a game of it if you have to live with it. We of S.P.L.A.T. have published a booklet on how to identify two hundred and thirty-four varieties of puppy poop, and we'd be glad to send it to anyone who . . ."

"I'm sorry, but that old clock on the wall tells us that we've run out of time."

Allen smiled at the audience. "Our guests today have been Malcolm Boyd, whose new record *Malcolm Boyd Wrestles with the Devil Accompanied by the Harmonicats, Recorded Live at the Holly-*

wood Brown Derby has just been released on Pious Pelf Records; David Susskind whose program 'Open End' is seen on over nine thousand television stations and digs deeply into Today's vital problems, and Jean Shepherd, the dynamic militant president of S.P.L.A.T., the Society for the Prevention and Limitation of Animal Turds. It's been a good show, hasn't it, folks?"

The crowd roared.

"Next week we take up the problem of drug addiction among prenatal infants, and . . ."

I awoke in a cold sweat; lay for a moment on my Castro. It had grown dark. The apartment was deep in gloom. A fetid breath of hot air drifted in from the street. I sniffed appreciatively.

"Ah, there's a rare one for New York. A Rhodesian Ridgeback!" I arose to pour myself another drink.

II

43 Miles on the Gauge

ROSSIE, IOWA (UPI) *(News Item)*
A treasure of antique automobiles, including one of the rarest vehicles known, has been discovered on a farm near here. The 23 autos were discovered by three men on the farm owned by the late Leopold Brown. The vehicles, vintage models, ranged from 1905 to 1951. Included in the find was a 1905 Winton touring car which antique buffs say is one of the two known to exist. The men said the cars were stored in boarded-up barns and sheds, and seven were found in a grove of trees. Some cars were buried up to their axles in dirt, and others were covered by underbrush. The find included a 1926 and 1927 Whippet coupe and a 1919 Hudson Six roadster. Oddly enough, there was also a 1951 Chevrolet with Power Glide, rare because it has only 43 miles recorded on the odometer.

Somewhere in J. D. Salinger's *The Catcher in the Rye* Holden Caulfield, the arch teen-age anti-hero, remarks that he once read a book and had an overwhelming desire to meet the author. Well, that's all right, I suppose, as far as it goes, but let's face it, fellow victims, authors write books and create fiction peopled by figures of the imagination, men who never were. There ain't no Yossarian. Ahab sailed on the poop deck of a ghostly, non-existent Pequod, and even James Bond was made of the sheerest pulp. But there *was* a Leopold Brown who walked this earth, thought his mysterious thoughts and dreamed dreams far beyond the reach of any character ever invented by Philip Roth.

Car collectors everywhere, reading that tiny item detailing Leopold Brown's spectacular backyard, can't help but feel a tightening around the throat and a shortness of breath caused by intense visceral excitement. Holy mother of God, a 1905 Winton Tourer *and* a 1951 Chevy (Power Glide) with 43 tiny miles on the gauge. For twenty years that Chevrolet (Power Glide) has rested amid the weeds cowl-to-cowl with a 1927 Whippet Coupe. Within winking distance, a jaunty 1919 Hudson Six roadster. It's one thing to collect old cars because they are old cars, and some guys just have a compulsion to glom onto anything that has even a hint of the antique about it; pop bottles, coffee grinders, horse collars, trombones, stuffed goats. But it is a totally different thing to deliberately go out and plunk down a couple of thousand good ones for a new Chevy, drive it back home to the farm and park it next to the Whippet to add to the good old collection. From all the evidence, the 1951 Chevy was never driven again after the day it left the dealer's!

Personally, you guys who would like to meet in the flesh Yossarian or Holden Caulfield are welcome to them. Both are staid, straight-laced unimaginative ciphers compared to the late Leopold Brown. A man capable of stashing away what he did in his back yard, without apparently making much noise about it, was a guy obviously capable of a hell of a lot more in his life that is not recorded in that brief newsnote.

I was squatting patiently on one of the plush settees at Mister Toni's, an elegant *salon de coiffure* in the heart of the high-rent district on Lexington Avenue when I came across the enigmatic newsnote that dealt with the late Leopold. Mister Toni's

211

used to be called Tony Mozzarella's Barber Shop just a few semesters back and featured heavily-jowled white-coated balding men who breathed garlic down your neck and told you dirty stories while they skinned your onion. Things are different now, and old Tony has not only changed the spelling of his name, but the entire atmosphere of the joint has become redolent of rare perfumes. The swish of hairnets competes with the hum of permanent wave machines. The stylists; wasp-waisted, gentle boys flutter about each chair, making fluting noises and speaking in sibilant lisps. So naturally I caused a little stir when involuntarily I barked, "Holy Christ Almighty, a *Hudson Six!!*"

Realizing immediately that Toni's was no place to discuss things of the real world that dealt with the affairs of genuine men, I quickly returned to *Gentleman's Quarterly* and its continuing discussion of the place of Belgian lace in the well-dressed man's attire. But I couldn't shake Leopold Brown out of my mind.

A few hours later, struggling up Broadway in a driving rain, on foot naturally since no self-respecting New York hackie ever ventures out into weather more sinister than a slight mist, I passed the new car showrooms that infest the area around 57th Street. There in the window of the Ford agency were a pair of new Pintos. Across the street I could see dimly through the driving rain a sparkling new Plymouth Duster. Not far away, enshrined in glass, there was a steel-grey Electra. Maybe it was the rain, or the wind, or the aftermath of the heady, expensive two hours at Mister Toni's, but Leopold Brown popped back into the quagmire I call a mind. Is there one among us who could dare to do what Leopold did? I doubt it. Men of his style just don't exist today. Which of these cars would Leopold have chosen for immortality? The Pinto? I doubt it. The Electra? Hardly. The Plymouth Duster? Don't be silly. The reason none of these fit exactly is because it is obvious that the late Leopold Brown was a genius. The mind of the genius always walks alone in solitary, unapplauded splendor. The world totters at the feet of such as Johnny Carson or Dick Cavett, while resolutely ignoring the likes of Leopold Brown. It was always thus; it will always be thus. True genius is a frightening and enigmatic thing. What makes the late Leopold Brown unique is his totally inspired choice of a 1951 Chevrolet (Power Glide) for preservation and immortality. The very mundane-ity, the staggering ordinariness of the 1951 Chevrolet (Power Glide) is the hallmark of Mr. Brown's blinding talent.

Unfortunately, the small news item does not list the rest of his selections; merely the Winton, the Hudson Six, the Whippet and the Chevy. There is a unifying theme here, and any truly serious student of automotive trivia can spot it instantly. What is it? As the rains battered against what was left of my shredded pliofilm Edwardian raincoat (naturally it was shredded, since I had already worn it for better than forty minutes and it was nearing the end of its life) it hit me like an illuminating flash, the same thing that used to happen to guys in the comics when that 60 watt Mazda switched on over Andy Gump's noggin. Of course! Now I saw it!

Leopold Brown's collection, *en toto*, was his legacy, his statement to the world. Think about it. A Whippet, a Hudson Six, a Winton, AND — a master stroke — a 1951 Chevrolet (Power Glide)! These cars have one characteristic in common. Each one was a stupefying Nothing of its day. The reason no Wintons exist is because the 1905 Winton was a colossal dud of that year. It had all the endearing qualities of a covered wagon powered by a rubber band, steerable only by heavily-muscled stevedores on the rare occasions when it actually ran. Leopold Brown obviously realized that the Winton (1905) represented more than a car for its day. The 1919 Hudson Six was another thudder, not anywhere near its contemporaries such as the Stutzes and the Lincolns of the day but yet not a total bomb. Somewhere in that great grey misty area of anonymous mediocrity, the Whippet 1927 vintage speaks for itself and of course it would take someone like a Leopold Brown to see (*at the time!*) that a 1951 Chevrolet (Power Glide) belongs among the classics of the Lumpen Proletariat.

Try it yourself. Try to pick a showroom model of today that you would preserve to speak for our time. Keep in mind Brown's Law: "Neither the superb nor the ridiculous, but the unobtrusively mediocre speaketh for the men of the time." Don't rush to say: "Yeah! How 'bout one of them great Datsun 240s or one of them Vegas?" No, my friend, you betray the usual narrowness of mind of the museum curator who believes that the best Art of a time speaks for that time. It's a great game to play when you're waiting in line at the cleaners or seeing your life go up in smoke sitting in some reception room waiting for the blonde at the desk to tell you that Mr. Bullard will see you now. Just what car really does say it for our time, this year?

It's not as easy as you think. In the end it takes men of the stature of Leopold Brown to make such brilliant, incisive selections as he did. Like all men of genius, Brown must have had his troubles from the lesser men who surrounded him. I can see the scene now:

Characters:

LEOPOLD BROWN, a slight, somewhat paunchy man of late middle years, wearing rimless glasses and a perpetual slight frown.

CHEVROLET SALESMAN, a beefy, florid, hearty gentleman who resembles somewhat Lee J. Cobb. He has a rich voice and an Elk's tooth on a gold chain on his vest.

Scene:

A Chevrolet showroom 43 miles from Rossie, Iowa.

LEOPOLD BROWN enters through the swinging doors. Huge signs hang from the ceiling: "1951 THE year

for Chevy!" and "The 1951 Chevy
means Fun!"

(*We see scattered around the
walls pictures of Dinah Shore and the
slogan "See the USA in a Chevrolet,"
with musical notes encircling her
face.*)

SALESMAN: "Yessiree, nice day, it
sure is. Seen the new Chevy? Boy,
they really did it in Detroit this year.
Yessiree, that new . . ."

BROWN: (interrupting him) "Yep."
(His voice is low and purposeful.)

SALESMAN: "Uh . . . yep? Yep
what?"

BROWN: "Yep. I seen it. That's why
I'm here."

SALESMAN: "Beautiful, isn't it?
Magnificent car. Let me tell you, the
beauty of the new Chevy just
doesn't . . ."

BROWN: "Nope."

SALESMAN: (stunned) "Excuse me.
Did you say Nope?"

BROWN: "Yep, I said Nope. It ain't
beautiful. That's why I want one."

SALESMAN: "Er . . . hehehehehheh."
(He laughs a forced laugh at what he
thinks is Brown's little joke.) "You
want one. Well, we have a beautiful

new Golden Sunset Bronze, and the convertible like Dinah Shore rides has just come in. Now, I can show you our brochures, and . . ."

LEOPOLD BROWN: "I want a plain two-door Chevy with Power Glide. I want that one over there. With the bad color. And the plastic seat covers."

SALESMAN: "Yes sir, it just so happens I can make immediate delivery."

BROWN: "How much?"

SALESMAN: "That'll be one thousand nine-hundred and seventy-nine dollars and eighty-eight cents. And that includes, of course, the Power Glide. And you are really gonna enjoy driving this car. Let me tell you . . ."

BROWN: (interrupting, peeling off the exact amount in worn bills from his large wad. He puts eighty-eight cents down on the counter) "Nope. Ain't gonna drive it."

SALESMAN: "By George, that's a good one." (He slaps his knee.) "I'll have to tell the boys at the Rotary Club that one. That's a hot one. 'Ain't gonna drive it.' Yessir, Mr.

Brown, probably buying it for the wife, eh? Or your daughter? By George, that's a goodie."

BROWN: "Nope. Buyin' it for myself. Gimme the keys."

SALESMAN: (speaking slowly, as though to a small child) "Of course, Mr. Brown. Here are your keys. And since you're not going to drive it, I suggest . . ."

BROWN: "I know my business, son. Don't need no advice. Been buyin' cars for years. As long as she can make it to Rossie, that's all I need. It's forty-three miles on the dot, and I want to get back before dark."

SALESMAN: (handing Brown the keys) "Yessir, and er . . . ah . . . drive happy!"

(Without a word Brown drives car out of showroom and disappears into the dusk.)

SALESMAN: "Boy oh boy. We sure can grow 'em here in Iowa!"

It never changes. The man of vision and foresight is always alone. Leopold Brown, hail and farewell. There have been few like you.

12

The Great
Chicken-Clawed Chooser

I can tell you that no man can ever re-
ally understand how it feels to be a
woman! I can certainly say that!
— Militant Women's Lib
Spokesman,
"David Susskind Show"

I squatted in front of my 118-inch (total
area) color TV set, half dozing amid the
endless barrage of panel verbiage that
passes for relevant entertainment these
days when the remark about not being able
to understand how it feels to be a woman
came winging out like a silver bullet from
the Lone Ranger's .44, clean and true. By
god, that's true, I thought, yes, by George,
hits the mark exactly. No way I'll ever understand how it feels to be Jane Fonda or
Raquel Welch, or even Minnie Pearl.

I sipped a little of my Jim Beam and allowed the endless blather from the tube to
flow over me in warm engulfing waves. It

occurred to me briefly that the Bullshit Session, which used to be confined mostly to bars, and kitchens after the pinochle game, has now become a major art form, being packaged by William Morris and applauded by countless millions of my fellow knuckleheads who log thousands of hours in front of the tube yearly, just watching an endless stream of BS artists parade before us, all blatting on into the night, punctuated by Right Guard commercials and an occasional pitch for Purina Dog Chow. Nobody ever settles anything or convinces anyone but it goes on and on like the mighty Mississippi who don't do nuffin', jes' keeps rollin' along. I keep hoping that one day one of these interminable wrangles will finally go all the way. The way I see it it goes like this:

> CAVITT: "And what do you say about that, Mr. Cranshaw? Do you agree with Mr. Toadley?"
> CRANSHAW: (a heavily-jawed craggy-browed Professor of some sort) "What'd you say?"
> CAVITT: "Do you agree with Mr. Toadley on what he . . . ?"
> CRANSHAW: "Agree with that son of a bitch! Why, that bastard . . ."

(TOADLEY, *a short balding man wearing bifocals, leaps to his feet, knocking over Cavitt's coffee table in his headlong rush to get at Cranshaw, swinging wildly. He mutters an incoherent oath as Cranshaw, nimbly catching Toadley in the groin with his knee, ducks as the studio audience cheers wildly.*)
CAVITT: (shouting over the hubbub) "AND NOW A WORD FROM BUGLEMASTER BEER."
(*The screen goes to black.*)

Oh well. It'll never happen, since practically everybody on TV is a talker and not a do-er. It hit me, on second thought as the Women Libbers rattled on, that the crack about not being able to understand how it feels to be a woman was the first sensible thing I'd heard on television since Chet Huntley announced his retirement. There ain't no way to know how it feels to be a woman if you're a man, and conversely there just ain't no way for a woman to know how it feels to be male.

Take the Great Chicken-Clawed Chooser, for example. There is hardly a man alive today who has not felt the sting, the humiliation visited upon the male by that evil bird. Why, hardly a female even knows what the term "Chicken Claws" means. *Chicken Claws!* Even now that mystic, cabalistic sinister phrase sends faint shivers of fear and apprehension running up and down the spines of millions of males who were never chosen.

From the time they begin to walk, males just naturally get involved in competitive games of all types and varieties, ranging from kicking a tin can around the street to throwing little sticks up in the air to seeing who can pee the highest up a garage wall. Now you can yell all you want about "they are taught by an evil, competitive, rotten, decadent Society, blah blah blah, bullshit bullshit bullshit," the usual claptrap that you hear around PTA meetings and Ad Hoc committees to stamp out capguns and catchers' mitts, but the fact is no matter where you go on the face of the earth, under whatever system or culture you can find, males try to see who can throw the dingdong the furthest, catch the kangaroo the quickest, stay under water the longest, harpoon the most seals or dry and shrink the most Baptist heads. Like Walter Cronkite says so endearingly: "Don't get mad. I don't make the news; I just report it."

Over it all hangs the evil spectre of that gigantic gnarled age-old yellowed talon of that great Chicken-Clawed Chooser. As I heard that Women's Lib spokesman (although I guess the word spokes*man* is another example of creeping chauvinism but unfortunately "spokeswoman" rolls heavily off the tongue and has no beat to it, so spokesman will have to do), the brief image of one subtle aspect of how it feels to be a man came into what's left of my mind. Could I explain to her how many raggletaggle male kids have stood knee-deep in the weeds back of a dusty First Base made out of an old beaten-up flour sack filled with sand as the Chicken-Clawed Chooser went about its inexorable work, cleanly and with deadly truth and efficiency. It is a hard fact, girls, but in every group of males larger than three, there are two who are just naturally the ones who do the choosing in any games and then there are the others, the motley band of those who hope to *be* chosen. It is hard to explain how a chooser becomes a chooser. He is not necessarily the largest or even the swiftest. It is something in the eye; a way of being, a steely, smoky gaze and natural talent, that most accursed of undemocratic human qualities that singles the chooser out from the shuffling pack. They almost always are named Mike or Al; short, clean, hairy names, to the point, no horsing around. Few Clarences are ever choosers. I, personally, have never known a Delbert who was ever allowed to choose anything. Maybe God, or the Life Force or whatever the hell it is knows even before birth that the genes have come together to create another chooser, and his parents — guided by a power over which they have no control — invariably name that tiny blob of human protoplasm correctly: Al. He's a born Al. And little Al, peering out of his crib with an embryonic smoky gaze of disdain, is launched into the world fully prepared to deal with the lesser fry.

Let's face it, when a school of fish, simple dim-witted carp, swim by aimlessly, there are one or two carp who are always in the van. How are they chosen? Is it an evil, decadent system that brought them there? Is it poor toilet training? Is it Chapter Ten in Doctor Spock? No. It is the Chicken-Clawed Chooser.

How does it work in actual combat, the nuts and bolts, or the mechanics of separating the sheep from the goats; the choosers from the rest? Our scene is laid on a Saturday morning. A crude ball diamond sprawls over a vacant lot. Gathered for the purpose of engaging in the sport of Roundball ("Bowls" it is sometimes called, more commonly termed "American base-ball") eleven males have assembled, all around the age of twelve. To the untrained observer they look almost identical, as to all but the most discerning eye a band of Polynesians in a puberty rite tend to be in-distinguishable one from the other. But be-lieve me, if you are or ever were one of them you know there are vast differences.

Al, a short broad-shouldered specimen wearing a dirty T-shirt, flips a bat toward Mike. Mike, slightly taller but narrower, has slit eyes and a Band-Aid covering a cut on his right cheekbone. Mike catches the bat adeptly at the trademark; holds it up-right while the others look on silently, si-dling back and forth unconcernedly. Do not be fooled. They are deeply involved and already fear is beginning to strike deep in the vitals of at least three of the on-lookers.

Al's hand grasps the bat tightly above Mike's. Hand by hand they work their way up the bat toward the narrow taped handle. Finally the top is reached. Al's hand is the last around the handle. There is a momentary pause. Mike barks:

"CHICKEN CLAWS." Al spits into the dust.

Al: "How come you didn't holler that before, you son of a bitch?"

Mike's hand has formed a claw and is grasping the very tip of the bat, just above Al's in a chicken-clawed grasp.

"You didn't say we couldn't have Chicken Claws," Mike grunts. These two have been choosing up for years. Their battles as to who gets the first choice have see-sawed back and forth over dozens of playgrounds.

"Okay, Mike," Al concedes reluctantly. The bat is tossed into the dust next to First Base and now the two turn to face the others, who shift from foot to foot, awaiting the blow.

"Okay. I'll take Gus."

Gus, at twelve, is six feet three. He weighs seventy-six pounds. He will never be a chooser but he will always, throughout life, be the first chosen. His natural fielding ability and his sullen competence at the plate are a by-word among his peers. He will never get the Prom Queen but will invariably nail at least three of her attendants. Gus will do all right. Gus picks up his glove and moves back of Mike. Already the team is being formed.

Al looks at the assemblage narrowly and finally barks:

"Stan."

Stan is almost in the same class as Gus, but not quite. His speed is legendary. He is a maniacal in-fighter and while not outstandingly gifted, his single-minded perseverance and the fact that his father owns a large chain of hardware stores will always stand him in good stead. Stan already, at the age of twelve, is a latent Vice President.

"Awright," Mike counters. Without hesitation he hisses:

"Dumpy."

Dumpy has always been chosen immediately after Stan, and occasionally even ahead of him. His nickname is derived from his family name of Dumplemeyer. He is not dumpy, being heavily muscled, narrow of waist and long of arm. However, he is somewhat dim-witted. In spite of excellent coordination he has a marked tendency to throw to the wrong base and was even known once to fall asleep in the outfield, with disastrous results. Dumpy will go through life continually impressing people with his promise, which never materializes. But that is enough in the Corporate world since Parkinson's Law of ineptitude will push him steadily upward. His fine profile; the way a blazer hangs on his frame will be enough for Dumpy. Weep no tears for old Dumplemeyer. He once in a great while hits a hell of a long ball.

Al glances back at his team. Stan, his only declared ally, picks his nose casually, waiting for the action to begin. Al examines the remaining six.

Al: "Lemme see. Okay. C'mon over here, Cliff."

Cliff is a special case, a true in-and-outer but in a sinister way. He has Mother trouble. Cliff's mother rides on his back like a winged vulture, constantly calling him home at crucial moments in ball games. While actually playing, he has a high level of competence, but his mother's watchword is "You'll get hurt playing with that hard ball!" Cliff will ultimately be somebody's bookkeeper. He will marry a large overbearing lady who will bear him many children. He will be a good bookkeeper but will be inclined to be plagued by psychosomatic colds, which his wife will blame on his alleged refusal to "wear rubbers and eat decent." Al would not have chosen Cliff had he not been getting down near the bottom of the barrel.

Mike carefully unpeels a wad of Fleers

229

bubblegum before making his choice. It is getting more difficult man by man. He pauses silently, causing the remaining five to twitch visibly.

"Aw . . . right. Make it Jeff."

Jeff, at twelve, five-foot-three, weighs two hundred and thirty-six. Slow of foot, dull of mind, Jeff is a natural catcher. Jeff ultimately makes every team he goes out for, just barely. His bulk carries him through. Kids bounce off him like hailstones. However, in spite of his size he is a notably poor hitter, and his position in life is strictly Defensive. It is almost impossible to reach the plate when Jeff is squatting like a rubber Buddha with an inhumanly low center of gravity. Throughout life he will be known as "good old Jeff" and will be sent continually for more beer at parties and will be useful for pushing the car and all the other basic tasks that man falls heir to. Jeff is a born Pfc., which he will later be, and will spend a lot of time on Guard duty and washing trucks in the Motor Pool. He will eventually become Assistant Night Foreman in the Shipping Department of Amalgamated.

Al, who obviously is disappointed at not getting Jeff, the best of a bad lot, looks the field over casually. The rest of the choices are really academic.

"Okay. I'll take Murphy."

Poor little Murphy, who really believes he can play baseball. Throughout life he will relentlessly pursue a variety of sports, attacking them with a dedicated frenzied total ineptitude. He will ultimately take lessons in golf, tennis, fencing, skiing, and whatever happens to be In at the moment. He also will be the only one of the crowd who will go to "swinging singles" weekends in the Catskills, will haunt Singles' bars on the East Side and will finally resort to Computer Dating. Murphy will paste Playboy bunny insignias on the windshield of his Pontiac GTO and will not have a serious involvement with a female till late in his 37th year. He will spend a lot of time and money buying ski sweaters, sun goggles, Arnold Palmer putters and books entitled *The Sensuous Man*, or *How To Make Love* (with four LPs and associated diagrams).

There are now three left. Without hesitation Mike, with a note of conciliation in his voice, lays out a proposal to Al. It is a chilling one but totally realistic. Ball games are to be won. Mike intends to win. There is no time for sentiment when the Great Chicken-Clawed Chooser is making his rounds. Like Death, he plays no favorites and Democracy means nothing to him. Who knows where he will strike?

"Look, Al, I'll take Howie if you'll take Marty and Clarence."

Al is visibly outraged. "Marty *and* Clarence! Fer Chrissake! This has happened to me three weeks in a row. I'll tell ya what. I'll take Marty and Clarence if you let us bat first."

This trio; Howie, Marty and Clarence, are virtually indistinguishable one from the other. Thin, weedy, bespectacled — at the age of twelve all three are noticeably balding. Howie scurries happily to Mike's side, nuzzling up to him contentedly. Totally lacking in coordination, his attempts at fielding have produced results so comical that he has taken refuge in a sense of humor, believing that if he can keep those around him laughing they will not realize that he is truly one of the Untouchables. His sallow skin, his weak watery eyes, his prominent teeth have made him the obvious butt of many of coarse jest. Howie will fantasize throughout his life that he is well-liked, since everyone laughs at his gags, but he secretly fears that no one has even noticed that he has left the room. He is right. However, if he gets a good agent he could go all the way. Nightclubs, movies, the works, at which point he will have a golf tournament named after him — "The Howie Desert Invitational" and guys like Jack Nicklaus will pretend that they're his friend. It will be plenty enough for Howie.

Marty and Clarence, while they may appear alike to the observer, are vastly different. Marty, by his thirteenth year, will no longer have much to do with anything that smacks of Sport. His complete inability to get anywhere near a rolling or bouncing ball and his abject fear of failure will lead him to becoming a zealous member of the Biology Club and the Hi-Y. He will later, as an adult, make vague statements that he believes contact sports are barbarous, but he won't really believe it since he will go through life as a silent fan, watching football players on television tubes, following Tom Seaver on Sunday afternoons, quietly regretting his incompetence. He will hurt no one.

Clarence, at twelve, still believes he has talent, because he did once, early last summer, actually snag a flyball. But the awful truth is beginning to dawn. Intensely intelligent, with an incredible ego, Clarence has been told from childhood that there are no such things as untalented children. There are just those whose real talents have never been brought out. He is finding otherwise and takes the pill bitterly. Already he is forming an intense hatred of Gus and his easy grace; of Mike and his level, lethal swing; of Al and his inhuman fastball. It is hatred tinged with intense envy. He will later become a novelist or playwright, and all through college will loudly entertain the fiction that all athletes are "jocks" and not worthy of the slightest

fleeting thought from one of the truly important people on the campus, that little happy band of scribblers on the *Literary Quarterly* and who dominate the Yearbook or the Humor Magazine with their brilliant wit. Later, after he has become rich and famous, he will seek the company of resoundingly successful jocks, at last being allowed into their Olympian presence. As Mailer courts middleweight boxers and Plimpton fawns on hulking linebackers, so will Clarence.

The players scatter to their positions. Marty suffers the ultimate humiliation, being assigned to Right Field to lurk patiently amid the tall grass where balls are seldom hit. The game begins, a languorous Saturday afternoon competition played out amid the rusting beer cans and Coke bottles of kiddom. Has Gloria Steinem ever been part of a package deal with Howie and Clarence? I doubt it. Has Germaine Greer faced Al's whistling slider and the scorn of Mike's curled lip? I doubt it. These are things that only the male ex-kid can well and truly understand.

The Great Chicken-Clawed Chooser knows. He cannot be fooled nor escaped. Some got it and some ain't. There's no way to tell a woman how it feels to stand in the presence of the Great Chooser and see his claws work inexorably up the bat, and there is no escape in the brilliant light of Truth. You can either go to your left, or you can't.

13

The Drive-In Confessional

News item:

QUARRYVILLE, PA. (UPI) *Small foreign car doubles as a confessional for Fr. John Campion, pastor of St. Catherine Of Sienna, Quarryville, Pa. on Saturday evenings during the summer when he hears confessions at the Muddy Run Campgrounds near his parish.*

I read the caption under the photo a couple of times to let the thought really sink in. The accompanying photo showed the good Father in full regalia, seated solemnly in his "foreign car," fittingly, a Fiat. A drive-in confessional, I thought. Well, it had to happen. The car has long ago ceased to be a status symbol, and in fact *not* owning a car has become some sort of distinction in this age of total wheels. I skimmed through the Sports page on my way back to the cross-word puzzle when 'way down near the back of the paper, amid the ads for trusses and $2.00 tax accountants, I saw this small item:

MAN BURIED IN CAR

IPSWICH, ENGLAND (REUTERS) *John Aldershot, 82, was buried today seated bolt upright at the wheel of his vintage Austin Seven. In his will Mr. Aldershot stated "She's been more faithful to me than any woman. In fact, I never found any faithful women in my whole life. No one else will ever own her. She's been my only friend." It was stipulated in Mr. Aldershot's will that he be buried at the wheel.*

Holy cow, I thought, quoting the great Phil Rizzuto, that's going to make one hell of a find for some lucky anthropologist a couple of thousand years from now. We're getting back to the style of the ancient Pharaohs, who are always tucked away fully-equipped with their favorite barge and maybe even a concubine or two.

This is the way my mind works some mornings when I've gotten up too early after having gotten to bed too late the night before, and the coffee tastes sourish and I feel Manhattan closing in. On the back page of the paper, I scanned a lush Pontiac ad that hinted that the buyer could achieve immortality, quite possibly live forever in a "totally controlled interior atmosphere" if he traded in his old, totally inadequate last year's model which had only promised him Everlasting Youth, for this year's dream machine. I took another pull at the lukewarm black coffee, trying gamely to pull my wits together. Drive-in confessionals, The Austin Seven crypt. Pontiac immortality. My mind quivered nervously, as it so often does these days, contemplating, indeed savoring, the blossoming role that the automobile has assumed. By God, there are beginning to appear distinct Religious overtones to the good old family sedan. As I shaved, and glared back at the soapy-faced stranger who peered out of the mirror at me, I noticed he seemed to be playing a ramshackle version of Scrooge. Thinking of drive-in confessionals too early in the morning can do that to you.

On my way to midtown, cradled deep in the bosom of Mother IRT, after I had read all the subway ads for Clairol, Ronzoni Spaghetti Sauce, L&M cigarettes and several thousand scrawled fragments of graffiti, all variations on the "Screw Whitey" theme, my mind began to wander. I pictured the scene at the drive-in confessional thusly:

Hangdog driver nattily attired in red white and blue bells, Boone Farm Apple Wine T-shirt and Stirling Moss driving gloves tools up to tastefully-designed stainless steel arch set by the roadside, arcing over the curving drive. It is surmounted by a stainless steel cross. Embossed on it is the legend SAINT ESSO — THE LITTLE CHURCH BY THE HIGHWAY. An electric eye clangs loudly as he drives under the arch. The sign reads TAKE TICKET FROM MACHINE BEFORE PROCEEDING. He reaches out of the cockpit of his Lotus Elan, grabs the ticket with a shaking hand, and drives on. He pulls into line behind an older Jaguar Mark 7 sedan. Several other cars are ahead of the Jag. A sombre black Fiat is parked amid the greenery. The driver of the car at the head of the line is talking frantically to the occupant of the Fiat. He appears to be crying. Time inches by as car after car takes its turn next to the consecrated 124. Finally, our driver wheels his Elan into position.

DRIVER: (gunning his motor several

times for reassurance) "Bless me, Father, for I have sinned."

PRIEST: "Yes, my son. And how have you sinned?" (He bends over his steering wheel, adjusting the knobs on his stereo tape deck which is quietly playing an organ version of *Ave Maria*.)

DRIVER: (his voice shaky with contrition) "I have committed adultery, Father. With my buddy Howie's wife."

PRIEST: "We are all too human. In these difficult times, such things cannot be avoided. That will be two Hail Marys and one Our Father."

DRIVER: "Thank you, Father. I will try not to do it again. But she is sure some dish!"

PRIEST: "The will is stronger than the body, my son. One can only try." (The line of cars behind the Lotus has lengthened mightily and a few impatient sinners have begun to toot their horns, calling for faster service.)

PRIEST: "Is that all, my son?"

DRIVER: "No, Father, I wish it were, but there's more. I . . . well, I . . . thought several evil thoughts about a

241

young lady in the Steno pool at the office, and Father . . ." (He trails off into an embarrassed silence.)

PRIEST: "The Devil takes many forms, and he is always present. Try to think these thoughts no more, my son. Peace of mind will ensue."

DRIVER: "Thank you, Father. They fired her last week anyway, so I guess I'm safe. Father, I don't know how to say this, but there is more, a lot more."

PRIEST: "One moment, son." (He removes the cassette from the tape-deck and replaces it with another. The solemn tones of a Gregorian chant recorded in some vast cathedral fill the Fiat.)

PRIEST: "You have had a busy week, if I may say so."

DRIVER: "I am sorry to admit that I have committed several Mortal sins."

PRIEST: "Several?"

DRIVER: "Yes." (Involuntarily he nervously guns the Lotus, sending up a billow of blue exhaust into the cockpit of the MGB behind him. The occupant, a thin bleached-blonde, protests coughingly amid the fumes. Several angry horns are heard again. Overhead, a 747 jet whistles by, carrying a crowd of merrymakers to Las Vegas. A Good Humor man, his bell ringing merrily, can be seen doing a brisk business with the waiting confessees in the line of cars.)

DRIVER: "Father, I failed to change the oil in the Lotus again."

PRIEST: "What? Again? I thought we were going to turn over a new leaf."

DRIVER: "I tried. I really did. But it slipped my mind."

PRIEST: (sternly) "That is no excuse. That will be five Hail Marys and three Our Fathers."

DRIVER: "I'm no good."

PRIEST: "Every man can be saved. Remember, five Hail Marys and three Our Fathers. There is still hope."

DRIVER: "No, Father, there isn't. All is lost!" (He begins to sob, his head dropping to the steering wheel, causing his horn to blow. He sobs on unheedingly.)

PRIEST: "There, there, my son. I have heard worse through this very window. You are but one among many." (He adjusts the Gregorian chants, which have become somewhat insistent.)

DRIVER: "No, Father. I am not one among many. I haven't told you the worst."

PRIEST: "What? There's more? You have indeed strayed."

DRIVER: (sweating profusely, eyes rolling wildly) "Father, I . . ." (gasping) ". . . BURNT OUT THE BEARINGS!"

PRIEST: (after hurriedly crossing himself, his face drawn and pale with horror) "Pray with me. Our Father who art in Heaven, forgive your son who hath sinned, for he knoweth not what he does. Amen." (The Driver mutters the prayer incoherently.)

PRIEST: "There is no absolution for a Mortal sin such as you have committed. We can only pray for God's forgiveness. I can promise you nothing. However, we must try to make amends. That will be fifty Hail Marys and twenty-five Our Fathers, and I would suggest a sizeable donation to our Driveway Renewal Fund."

DRIVER: "I was afraid of excommunication. It won't happen again."

PRIEST: "Your time is up. May I have your ticket, please." (The driver hands him his ticket, which is punched by the priest and filed in his glove compartment. The driver puts the Lotus into gear and drives off, trailing a cloud of blue smoke. The MGB, its occupant sobbing, wheels into place.)

BLONDE: "Bless me Father, for I have sinned. . . ."

I clung to the hanging strap of the swaying subway car, enjoying my little drama. The next step, I thought, of course would be drive-in Baptisms, drive-in marriages and who knows where it could lead; maybe deacons on Hondas, and the collection plate would be a toll house with an EXACT CHANGE lane. Once this kind of thinking gets hold of you, you can hardly stop. Out in California they've already got drive-in mortuaries where the deceased is laid out in a glass case wearing his favorite costume from life, his surfers maybe or his tie-dyed jeans, and his friends come tooling up and pay their respects without ever having to get out of the Buick.

That's one of the great things about subway life; it's one of the few times when a guy really stares long and hard at his own navel. The one thing you better not do, ever, is catch the eye of somebody else in the car, that is, if you value the health of your liver, since a casual glance can easily precipitate a major knife fight or worse. So the experienced twentieth century man-mole, the subway rider, becomes adept at an Urban form of Yoga mind-suspension. I realize it is not fair to spring it on you out-landers like this, but have you ever won-dered why most of the earth-shaking plays, novels, poetry, graffiti, and other major art forms reach their fullest flower in New York? Hardly anybody ever writes a decent novel out of Goshen, Indiana, or Pebble Lake, Minnesota, and I submit it's because they have no subways where a man is forced daily to deal with the raging fires of Evil and fantasy which lie in the guts of all of us. It's just that people Out There where the sun shines and Simoniz still works can afford to ignore the nether regions and get away with it. It is during my strap-hanging sessions that I get some of my worst de-structive, often cataclysmic visions, so I'm hanging there thinking about drive-in con-fessionals, the sinner in my fantasy Lotus, wondering what the blonde in the MGB pulled off that made her so nervous and whether or not the Father in the Fiat would eventually make Bishop and be awarded, maybe, an Alfa by the Vatican, when I catch sight of Miss Subways staring fixedly although somewhat blankly out of a subway ad directly in front of me.

MISS SUBWAYS for this month is Marcia Bugleblast. Marcia is a clerk-typist at the Continental Burial Urn Corporation in Long Island City. Her hobbies are playing the piano, collecting ceramic giraffes and motoring with friends. She hopes to go into TV and is studying Acting at the Mme. Ester Klooberman Dramatic Studios on Utopia Parkway.

Marcia appeared to be wearing a rubber wig in the photograph, which had been suitably mutilated by the roving bands of Folk Artists who infest the Seventh Avenue line. "Motoring with her friends." Golly Ned, I thought, I haven't heard that expression since I gave up reading the *White Castle News*, which as any good hamburger hound knows is distributed along with sliced pickles and fried onions at all the White Castles of the Midwest.

A blast of ripe air swept through the straphanging mob as our car paused briefly at 34th Street where it disgorged a mob of Macy maniacs hurrying single-mindedly toward yet another White Sale. Briefly I pictured Marcia Bugleblast and her friends "motoring" through the Jersey junkyards in a grape-colored '53 Ford Galaxie, the very picture of elegance and twentieth century leisure living. Suddenly I spotted a seat vacant. Not really a seat, but a small, unoccupied crevice between a large Puerto Rican lady festooned with so many kids they seemed to come in bunches like thousands of squalling, sticky grapes. On the other side of the crevice was a thin, parchment-skinned, wiry native wearing a straw hat that would have gotten him twenty-five bucks easy in any antique shop and reading a Gideon bible probably stolen from some wayside Howard Johnson Motor Inn, since he was using the celluloid DO NOT DISTURB sign for a bookmark. Darting forward like a sweaty eel I slithered into the tiny crack between my fellow human beings.

The car started to move, and again my mind jumped a cog and began to wander . . . Drive-In confessionals . . .

248

Marcia Bugleblast motoring with her friends . . . John Aldershot and his Austin crypt . . . I wondered if . . . ?

14

The Indy 500

The 500? The True Believers are in the Infield guzzling beer, playing pinochle and celebrating a unique Religious rite.

"Fer Chrissake, Carl, don't forget the goddamn bottle opener!"

My old man's voice floated through the pre-dawn darkness. "You outa yer mind?" my Uncle Carl answered, his voice sharpedged with scorn.

It was a ridiculous statement. My Uncle Carl had never been without a bottle opener since he was nine, and he didn't use the opener on Nehi Orange bottles either. The day, late in his eighth year, that he discovered beer was the day he discovered Life.

I lay in the blackness of my bedroom, listening to every golden word of the dialogue that was going on in the kitchen. Doors slammed; feet clumped up and down the back porch steps. Finally all was silent, except for the distinctive mutter and moan of a GM truck starter and an occasional muffled curse as the son of a bitch flooded again. Across the room my kid brother slept on peacefully, clutching his pink and blue Easter bunny. At last the sound of a motor finally catching; a couple of quick, bellowing roars to clear the valves of accumulated glop, and then the sound of the panel truck backing out of the driveway, the reverse gear shuddering painfully, and then finally the low murmuring hum as the True Believers disappeared into the night, heading straight South down U.S. 41. I lay in the blackness, unable to sleep, knowing that they had joined a great migrating horde of co-religionists heading toward Mecca, which lay a couple of hundred miles away on the Indiana plains; as flat, as featureless as the top of a Brunswick Bulky Collander billiard table.

The traumatic and moving experiences of Childhood are never truly forgotten, nor outlived. By God, the child *is* the father of the man. You can bitch all you want about it, you can shake your fist at the lowering heavens, you can pretend, posture, whistle in the dark, write a bad novel, all proving that you are far superior, more enlightened than the previous generation. If you'll ex-

251

cuse the expression — Bullshit! History, in spite of what Henry Ford said about it, will ultimately give you its inevitable kick in your egotistical ass.

My Old Man, my Drunken Uncle Carl and my Sneaky Uncle Al, although I doubt whether they suspected it, were part of a vast historical panoply. And the end is not yet in sight. The Old Man and his buddies were not religious men. I never heard my father use the Lord's name except in vain. God has been dead a lot longer than the editorialists in the *Time/Life* building would ever suspect. Like most of the Eastern Establishment, they are markedly and curiously behind the times. Long before Malcolm Boyd began his lucrative LP-cutting and Late Show Norman Vincent Peale-ing, the Old Man and practically everybody else in the vast underbelly of what had been the Bible Belt were already worshipping another God.

Like all religions, there were many sects, subdivisions, heretics, and, naturally, the Orthodox. My father believed all the way with the fervent, unselfconscious, total, honest commitment. He believed so thoroughly that he didn't even know he believed. It was as natural to him and his crowd as breathing. He believed in Oldsmobiles. The current Buick ad line: *Something to believe in — your Buick* would have sounded perfectly logical and honest to my father, except that he would have split a gut laughing because he hated Buicks, which he always associated with "Sunday drivers."

"Christ, look at the fat-assed Buick wallowin' around!" is the way he handled that sect.

Every serious religion has its Vatican, and from the earliest time I can remember the Vatican of the Indiana car nuts was that fateful, beautiful, violent brick rectangle known formally as the Indianapolis Motor Speedway. They always say you've got to be Italian to be a true Catholic. There is a great body of evidence that says you've got to be from Indiana to truly know and understand the 500. This is no mere bit of chauvinism. It is the literal truth. Indiana as the wellspring of creative Automobile genius will one day be, no doubt, the subject of a Ph.D. thesis. Fred and Augie Dusenberg's masterpiece, the magnificent Auburns, were not just cars, they were *Indiana* cars. The racing Studebakers out of South Bend were part of it too. Even today the Hoosier landscape is dotted with grizzled old codgers who ac-

253

tually built, with their own hands, boat-tailed speedsters and monster SJs. So it is natural that the track, which was originally conceived as a testing ground for these fire-eaters, would be — and is — more than just another race course. As Churchill Downs was once a track where elegant men competed in an effort to actually improve the breed, so the Indianapolis Motor Speedway was one of the few places on earth where manufacturers who made motor cars for ordinary driving-around people pitted them against their rivals in an effort to improve their breed. Howard Marmon was personally tangling with Fred and Augie when their cars boomed away for the start of the first 500 in 1911. His laconic chief engineer, who had helped design the car, Ray Harroun, tooled the big yellow Marmon, No. 32 painted on its vertical fin and called *The Wasp*, to victory in the first 500. He averaged just under 75 mph for the distance, and after it was over, said "I'll never drive another race again. Not for twice the money." He pocketed the fourteen grand and went back to his drawing board. Try to top that for cool, Andretti.

The air of Indiana is somehow permeated with the slit-eyed nonchalance of guys like Harroun. Wilbur Shaw, Bill Vukovich, Fred Frame, Jimmy Murphy, Howdy Wilcox, Doc Myers, Duke Nalon, Mauri Rose, the whole lot. It's like they all strode off a Republic Picture back lot in their coveralls, their goggles pushed up high on their cloth helmets, chewing tobacco and using short four-letter words liberally. Let's face it, the Indy — and by the way, no one who really knows the classic ever calls it the Indy: that phrase itself denotes profound ignorance of the tradition — the 500 is all you have to say. There *is* no other 500. It would be as if you called the Kentucky Derby the "Churchie" in your sad ignorance.

My Old Man, Uncle Carl and Uncle Al as they struggled south on U.S. 41 were only doing the natural thing. They never thought of it as a chic sporting event. They were heading for another 500, as naturally and as inevitably as a Catholic goes to church on Easter. It wasn't for a few years that I was allowed to come along, because it was one hell of a rough weekend. For three days or more the Old Man and his gang parked in line, a long serpentine procession of dust-covered hairy vehicles, waiting for the big shot at the Infield parking lot. Some guys had been in that line for two weeks.

They planned their whole year around this moment, scheduling their two week vacation in order to coincide with the 500. Ten days of their vacation they spent sitting on the running board of their Chevy, drinking beer, telling dirty stories, kicking the kids around, and waiting.

Over the years a whole tradition had built up around these waiting cars. Some of the cars were used only for this purpose, being kept in the back yard throughout the year like a flat-top in mothballs waiting for the next War. The Old Man, Uncle Carl and silent Al never gave a damn about being first in line. The important thing was just to *be* in line. The 500, unlike European races, is genuinely Masculine. Even the movie star who hands out the traditional victory kiss always looks a little embarrassed. The 500 is as remote from the Grand Prix de Monaco as a beer bust at Gus' Tavern on a Friday night is from a Sunday afternoon brunch at George Plimpton's. Plimpton will never quite understand it, and the vague sense of being intruders on a secret rite always plagues the Eastern writers as they try to "capture the elusive essence of the 500," as one so delicately put it recently.

All through the weekend of the race I

read all the stuff in the papers and looked at the pictures of the cars. For at least a month before Memorial Day every newspaper ran stories on the drivers and their magnificent racers with the great names: The Blue Crown Special, Zink Special, Maserati, and the fantastic Novi Specials. The night before the race the home town paper had a full section, eight or nine pages, devoted to nothing but individual pictures of the 33 drivers seated in the car each would take the pace lap in the next day. Next to his picture was the number of his starting position. A lot of these guys had raced at County Fairs, on dirt tracks all over the state, so they were more than just celebrities.

Hour after hour the race droned out of the radio. I knew that somewhere in that muttering mob, that cauldron of roars, the Old Man and Uncle Al were trying to keep Carl sober enough to watch the race. A couple of days after it was over they came roaring up the driveway, trailing blue smoke and slamming doors.

"Holy Christ, what a race!" was all the Old Man said as he plopped down at the kitchen table, his beet-red sunburned face somehow different from when he had left. It was over for another year.

★ ★ ★

"How'd you like to help with the driving down to Indianapolis this year?" my father casually remarked at supper one night late in April. In Indiana kids begin to drive at just about the time they can see over the steering wheel. They begin dreaming of getting their drivers' license at about the moment they learn the first four letters of the alphabet. Getting a driver's license in the Midwest was a little like being Confirmed, or maybe a Bar Mitzvah. At the age of ten I already had three solid years of driving behind me, naturally with the Old Man sitting next to me, and hollering all the while.

"Uh . . . y' mean the Race?"

My kid brother put down his fork with its impaled piece of meatloaf and began turning green.

"Yeah. We're takin' the Olds this year. Uncle Al has a bad back, so I thought you might help with the driving."

My mother, hanging over the stove in the background, said nothing, although her hair curlers rattled slightly. Going to the 500 was not something you did casually.

"I'm grindin' the valves on the Olds this weekend and I gotta go down to Sears and get some gaskets. Y' wanna go?"

All that weekend we ground the valves on the Cleveland Street Special, a second-hand Olds with worn kingpins.

"Yep, I figure this is Lou Meyer's year."

The Old Man rattled on as he mixed the valve-grinding compound, dripping sweat onto the back porch steps.

"That Bowes Special is really a pisser." He thought about this for a moment. ". . . Read about it in *Popular Mechanics*. Straight eight."

I said nothing, since I was in the novice class and I didn't want to rock the boat. All I wanted to do was *go!*

Every day this thing grew bigger and bigger, like some distant mushroom poking up out of the earth. I was going to the 500! Ever since I could remember I had been a real Indianapolis fanatic. I went to see *The Crowd Roars* at least forty times. Wherever it was playing, I was there. Contrast the insipid artiness of *Grand Prix* with that hairy classic and you'll see how far down the pike Western Civilization has gone. All that jazzy camerawork and Yves Montand mooning around Eva Marie Saint would probably make Kelly Pettillo want to puke. Jimmy Cagney, his oil-stained goggles, the rubber stripping off his rear wheels, his car in flames, was what Indianapolis was about, and if you think that's Fiction you don't know a damn thing about the race. Somehow I just can't see Jackie Stewart pushing his car down the straightaway after a flaming accident just to *finish*. Mario Andretti, possibly, but just possibly.

Day after day I scrounged through the papers, reading every tiny notice of what was going to happen at that Memorial Day's classic. Wilbur Shaw had a new Maserati, 183 inches. Chet Millers, Rex Mays and Floyd Roberts were all making fantastic predictions about how little chance the other drivers had. I ate up this stuff like a piranha breaking Lent. Every night at supper I'd bring it up, something I'd read in the *Chicago Tribune*.

"May drives good, but he's a blowhard," was a typical pre-race analysis from the Old Man.

"Watch Meyer. He *plans* a race. He doesn't just get out there and run like hell."

The Old Man was a Lou Meyer fan the way Madison Avenue junior executives dig Joe Namath. He could do no wrong. I didn't argue. After all, he had been going to the 500 since *he* was a kid and there's no sense arguing with history or City Hall.

Spring hits fast and sudden on the

flatlands of Indiana. One day there's snow and ice up to your posterior, with an ice-pick wind screaming off Lake Michigan and it feels like it won't be anything but grey rock ice and miserable-ness forever, and then zap — like some unbelievable miracle one day it's Spring. Everything melts; the sun is golden and guys start knocking out flies and chasing ground balls. There are usually three or four residual snowstorms, but you don't really take them seriously, even if they drop forty inches of snow.

It was a spectacular May, where every day was warmer and greater and more golden than the one before. Three days before Memorial Day, Uncle Carl, Al, the Old Man and I nosed out onto Route 41. The trunk was packed with everything from mustard to spare can openers. Inside the car we sat wedged between thermos bottles, blankets, comforters, folding camp chairs, a card table, and God-knows-what.

Ten miles out of town the Olds started to drift hard to the left, pulling toward the center line.

"Son of a *bitch!*" The Old Man banged on the wheel with his fist, blowing cigarette smoke through his nostrils like some really bugged dragon. We pulled off onto the shoulder and for the next fifteen minutes struggled with the jack. The sun hung overhead, beating down on the top of us as if it was trying to make up for all that winter.

"God dammit! It slipped again!" He was trying to line up the wheel nuts.

"Why don't you pretend it's a pit stop?" My Uncle Carl laughed and spit hard into the gravel.

"God dammit, if you're so smart why don't you help instead of standin' around cracking wise?"

Eventually we got the jack down, and the spare tire held. We rolled on, through cornfields just beginning to show green, with high-tension wires stretching off into the horizon.

Every time he had a flat the Old Man got moody for a while. He brooded about some Utopia where tires always had rubber. You didn't talk to him during this period. Uncle Al, however, didn't know this.

"Well, you should have heeded Barney Oldfield's advice," he said in a quiet sarcastic voice from the back seat.

"Who?" I asked. The Old Man remained silent.

"Barney Oldfield, my boy," said my

uncle, exuding superiority. "A famous race driver of the ancient past."

"Oh," I said, immediately bored. The ancient past holds no glories for budding youth.

"Okay, I'll bite," the Old Man said with a rising note of irritation in his voice. He didn't like to be interrupted while brooding.

"He had a famous phrase which was emblazoned on his car. It dealt specifically with the problem of flat tires."

"All right, wise guy, let's hear it." My father peered gloomily out of the window at a passing Bull Durham sign.

"My only life insurance is my Firestone tires."

"Oh fer Chrissake, what a load of crap!" My father snorted in disgust and spit out of the window. He was a Goodyear man.

We had cheeseburgers and rootbeer at a truck stop outside of West Lafayette and pushed on. Ahead of us a big Chrysler with an iron pipe rack on the roof rumbled steadily. Behind us a fenderless Chevy with a cracked windshield contained five blue-jowled 500 fans hurling beer cans at intervals into the cornfields.

Just as the day was ending we pulled into line to begin the Big Wait. It was all I'd heard, and more. Squad cars cruised up and down, watching for trouble. Bonfires broke out. A fat lady squatted on a wooden bench next to a Studebaker and breast fed a kid who looked like it was asleep. Uncle Carl went off to get ice for the beer.

That night I slept in the back seat, propped up in the corner between the card table, a big sack of hot dog rolls and my Uncle Al, who snored like the roars of a primeval beast.

The next morning I wandered up and down the line of cars, looking at the guys who wore jackets covered with patches showing they had been to 500s going back to the days when the Stutzes battled the Marmons. They sat around and played pinochle and sniffed a lot, the way old men do in the morning. Big Harley Davidsons and Indians roared up and down. The day wore on. Rumors floated back and forth.

"Joe Thorne just turned a fantastic practice lap."

"Billy DeVore has got a gut ache."

"Chet Gardner's having valve trouble."

The Old Man already had the admission tickets for the Infield. Everything was set now for action. The trunk was locked. Every movable thing was battened down. Final instructions were issued.

"Now look . . ." The Old Man tossed the car keys into the air, with his skull and crossbones keyring that he won at a raffle at the American Legion Hall.

". . . Now look, when that Dago bomb goes off I want all of you to be ready. I don't want anybody wandering off, because when that bomb goes off, I'm *going!* If you're out in the bushes takin' a leak or something, that's your hard luck. Any questions?"

Uncle Carl pried the top off another bottle of Atlas Prager.

"Could I help it last year 'cause I got a weak bladder?"

"It's all that goddamn beer." The Old Man scratched his rump.

"If you would hold off on the beer till we got into the Infield we'd make it easy."

"I always get nervous just before the bomb goes off. Then I gotta go." Uncle Carl was a truthful man.

"Well then, goddammit, take a milk bottle and pee in the car!" Being a 500 fan, like driving in the race itself, puts a severe test to the physical side of man. More than one driver has lost a couple of laps, and the race itself, because of a weak bladder. There is no point in mentioning names, but among the true *aficionados* there is a story of a famous driver pushing a seventy-five thousand dollar Offenhauser-powered Kurtis roadster for an owner who had his last cent invested in the car, when all of a sudden, eight laps to go and in the lead, Nature not only beckoned but began to press so insistently that he came into a turn too fast, trying to hold it back, and almost flipped over the wall. He whistled into the pit and tore off for the john. By the time he got back and into the cockpit, it was all over but the shouting. He had dropped back to third, and there was no chance to make it up.

"Fer Chrissake, why the hell didn't you go in yer pants? We just booted seventy grand right out the window!"

The owner could see his wife packing for the Poorhouse, and his kids selling the dog to raise carfare to get to the Orphan Home. The driver came back with what has now become a classic and is often quoted in the inner circles: "Gee, I never thought of *that!*"

All that night I didn't sleep a wink, and I guess nobody else did either. At 6:00 a.m. with the sun just coming up good, we sat around the Olds chewing on hot dog buns for breakfast and passing around a quart of lukewarm milk. The tension was getting unbearable. Up and down the line guys started their engines. You could hear them revving up again and again. The Old Man pulled out his Ingersoll.

"Seven minutes." He gunned the Olds. Time ticked on. 6:29:30 . . . BOOOOOM! KA-BOOOOOOOOOMMMMM!

The aerial bombs exploded high overhead, the same sound that had marked the opening of the first 500 back in the ancient primordial days of Ray Harroun and *The Wasp*. The line of cars roared forward in a great crunch of excitement and aggression. We lurched out. I got hit on the back of the neck by a loose thermos. The pain roared down my shoulderblades. I would feel that knock for years to come, although I didn't know it at the time. In a mad maelstrom of crashing metal, flailing fenders and swearing drivers we finally got through the gate and into the blessed historical Infield. Already it seemed to be mostly filled with families who had parked in the same spot since the days when cars carried mechanics and they had balloon races before the start of the 500.

It was now about nine o'clock and the sun was getting hot. All around me the great tapestry of Infield life began to take shape. Guys put together platforms made out of threaded pipe, with canvas canopies on the more elegant. They sat and teetered high above the earth like some strange race of stilted birds. Blankets were spread and the party began. The first pinochle games broke out here and there.

I stood on top of the roof of the Olds, peering through the spyglass I had bought from an ad in the Johnson/Smith catalog. A flash of yellow down near the grandstand. Holy Christ, it was a race car! I could see it clearly through the lens, bright yellow, low, with jet-black tires. Some guys in white coveralls were pushing it. Suddenly I heard from somewhere off to my right a low rumble. It grew louder. Just like on the radio! A red streak hurtled through my lens, past the yellow car.

Anyone who has heard the sound of an Offenhauser engine at speed will never forget it. The great crowd in the Infield eddied and surged with a life of its own. The sun grew hotter and hotter as the time for the race drew closer. From where we were, only a tiny sliver of track could be seen, but that was enough. I could see the heat waves rising from the surface of the track, and from time to time a car would streak through, leaving a blue haze behind it. That sound of *ooooooaaaannnngggg, oooo* when he decelerated in the turns and then *WWWWOOOOOOMP* coming out made the air vibrate.

From somewhere a PA system kept squawking incessantly. My Uncle Carl sat on the running board and strummed his banjo.

Yessir, that's my baby
No sir, don't mean maybe . . .

He sang between sucks at a beer bottle. The old man had out his race program and was writing things as they announced last-minute changes over the PA. A band struck up somewhere; some High School band paraded down the track. The pace car, a big white convertible, rolled out. The people cheered. I could hardly stand it. At last all thirty-three cars were lined up in that long, wild mosaic that is the traditional 500 start.

"Now listen careful, they're gonna say it pretty soon." The Old Man listened for the magic words that had been spoken in Indianapolis from the very beginning.

"GENTLEMEN, START YOUR ENGINES."

The PA system echoed the immortal words. I never thought I actually would hear them in person. A great roar spread out over the Infield as car after car revved over. Blue-grey smoke and the smell of burning exotic fuel made me almost pass out with excitement.

The pace car started to roll and the great parade roared by on the classical Pace Lap. They moved out of our sight. Balloons floated high up over the stands. Guys stood on hoods, fenders, rickety platforms, everything, to see the start, and when it came it was more than even I had imagined it to be.

BBBAAAAAARRRRROOOOOOOOO-MMMMM!

The earth trembled. Tires screamed. The crowd actually *did* roar! Just like the movie! I squinted through my glass as car after car streaked past the tiny sliver of track I could see. Blue, yellow, red, and a white blur that was Wilbur Shaw's Maserati. The race was on. And for ever and ever no one would be able to convince me that there is any more exciting a happening, and that's what it is, than the 500.

I've sipped chablis on an elegant balcony

overlooking the harbor at Monaco, and watched the finish from in the stands, right on the line, but somehow the whole spectacle is different. There is an animal, primitive thing about the 500.

The Infield was swinging into full action. Lunch baskets were opened, tablecloths spread, pickle jars spilled, pork and beans, fat ladies, skinny kids, old men in baseball caps, all sort of jammed up in one big compost heap of humanity.

The race droned on and on in the heat. Unless you're really damn lucky you don't see much of the race from the Infield. You hear it; you feel it; you eat it; you smell it. The PA system kept up a running tattoo of trivia and information. Jimmy Snyder in the Sparks Special, Lou Meyer in the Bowes Special and Wilbur Shaw were battling it out. Suddenly, from somewhere off in the distance, a dull *whuuummp* broke the steady drone. Instantly card games stopped; people leaped to the tops of cars. The yellow flag was out. For a while no one knew what happened, and finally the story reached even the ladies sitting in the shade eating ham sandwiches: Floyd Roberts had tangled with another car and had gone over the wall, and was dead.

The race began again. Finally, just about

the time I thought I'd pass out from heat and too much rootbeer, Wilbur Shaw took the checkered flag, and the ballgame was over. You couldn't have told it from where we were parked, but that's what the PA system said. Wilbur Shaw had done it again.

Guys began taking down their racks and packing away the baskets and card tables. It was getting late, and a lot of them had a long way to go before they got home, places like Olathe, Kansas; Red Cloud, Minnesota; and Turtle Creek, Iowa.

We finally got back out on 41, after dark and after the biggest traffic jam I ever saw in my life. I would, from that day on, always associate races with agonizing traffic jams. We droned northward between the same cornfields.

"Too bad about Roberts," my Uncle Al said in the dark. He never talked much, but when he did it wasn't often about cars.

"Yep," the Old Man answered, lighting up a cigarette as he hunched over the wheel.

"He won last year, but I guess his number come up. I always figure if your number comes up there's nothing you can do."

After making this Folk observation he

272

drove on in silence. I opened a Baby Ruth bar in the dark and chewed on it, thinking about what a great thing the 500 is, and how I'd tell everybody back home how I saw Floyd Roberts' car flip over the wall even though it was a lie.

"Wilbur Shaw in that goddamn Maserati." The Old Man said it as though he couldn't quite get over it.

"You know, I come to a conclusion . . ." He paused dramatically.

". . . Them damn Spaghetti-Eaters can really build fast cars!" The great race was over, and my Old Man had foretold the future.

15

Lifetime Guarantee

YOU *MUST* BE SATISFIED OR DOUBLE YOUR MONEY BACK! Ah, what a comfortable, reassuring, warming, cuddly phrase that is, a phrase probably more ubiquitous than any single slogan, motto, epithet, punchline; anything on the scene today. Whole political philosophies and theologies are based on one permutation of that line or another. It may be couched in cloudy Idealistic phrases such as:

"The right of all free men to live in harmony and peace, etc. etc., blah, blah, in hoc agricola conc . . ." or it may come in its more fragrant forms, such as an advertisement inviting you to live forever in Marlboro Country, which seems to have only strong, healthy, hungry-eyed, bronzed people of indeterminate Springtime youth existing forever in a land where there appear to be no buildings at all, only endless beautiful canyons and rugged, picturesque riding trails — certainly no used car lots or hospitals with cancer wards.

Or maybe you prefer Thunderbird Country, where no fenders are ever banged, no differentials ever fall out, and no greasy kids scratch:

"Wash me, you fathead!"

on the beautiful iridescent bronze rear deck.

The Double-Your-Money-Back, You-Must-Be-Satisfied, Guaranteed Syndrome is now galloping full blown through the great, vast empty spaces of the mind's vacuum of today's resolute Dreamer. He blames the rotten American system, a sick, decadent Society, for the fact that every girl he tries to make puts him down as a pimply-faced weed. No wonder he becomes a militant New Left zealot in the full blush of the Double Your Money Back Hangup. He believes that any planned, Totalitarian, guaranteed forever beautiful, lovely, Forever Singing Folksongs In The Wheatfields society must be preferable to the old Every-Man-For-Himself-And-Let-The-Weeds-Fall-Where-They-May Fordham Road world.

One knothead recently sued a local university here in New York indignantly proclaiming that after four years of toil he was still a notable lout at graduation time, a perfect example of the Satisfaction Guaranteed myth at its best.

"Four years at NYU and we guarantee that you will be wise, profound, brimming with wisdom and totally With It or double your money back!"

No wonder he became a Buddhist monk when after graduation he found that his lips still moved when he read the Want Ads in the *Daily News*.

The framers of our much-maligned Constitution were men of sterner stuff, and knew a hell of a lot more about Life as she is lived than the average graduate student today at CCNY, who gains much of his "knowledge" of existence from reading various items from the stacks and then filling out multiple choice questions on philosophical concepts of Cosmic complexity. You will note that line at the very beginning of the Constitution which guarantees you the right to *pursue* happiness. Nowhere is it even implied that you will ever catch up with that particular electric rabbit, or even glimpse it in the distance amid a cloud of dust.

Great numbers of parents today who have faithfully followed innumerable texts

guaranteed in one way or another to produce model offspring are dully throbbing
in lonely living rooms while Barbie or
Kenny slowly volplane around the chandelier at a pot party down the block.

"Where have we failed?" they moan. "We
followed every word to the letter in Dr.
Spock's golden book!"

Kids, on the other hand, are forever
being told that they, being Teenagers, are
magical beings closely related to elves, if
not outright nymphs and fairies, destined
forever to run along endless uncluttered
beaches, golden hair streaming in the
breeze, with the cry "SURF'S UP!" min-
gling with the Pepsi-Cola jingle. Instead,

they often find themselves short, notice-ably fat, near-sighted and with bad molars. Naturally, they feel someone has goofed up on their guarantee.

Whole nations are now in the thrall of this remarkable hangup. For fifty years they've been trying to make the Workers' Paradise paradisical. And still the suits are baggy, the underwear binds, mothers-in-law weep, guitar strings break, and the women are fat. The cry then goes up:

"Who screwed us!? It must be ——— !" Fill in the blanks. It's always somebody else. No one ever seems to question the concept of the guarantee itself.

Equality today is equated with happi-ness. We'll see.

The uproar will go on forever and ever. In fact, some are even going so far in pur-suit of the Double Your Money Back golden fleece as to arrive at that eventual poor old dead end and Scapegoat of all eternity — God. Already, in the last few months, there have been more and more editorials ranting and raving against a God everyone claims they don't believe in for doing such rotten stuff to *Us*, and using that argument to prove that's why they don't believe in Him, a classic example of the man who, six months after purchase, finds that Life itself is burning oil and getting lousy gas mileage.

Remember, gang, if you want to get ahead, just offer the mob a guaranteed, gold-plated, ribbon-bedecked Parchment, Scroll, White Paper, Manifesto, Constitution or what-have-you ensuring that if the instructions are carefully followed, Happiness, Satisfaction and the golden attainment of Peace of Mind will inevitably result. Whether you peddle creeds, dogmas or drugs, the mob will flock. It's only later that they will turn on you, but by then, we hope, you'll be living comfortably in Switzerland.

16

Moose Area Next 18 Miles

If you're a Saab cuckoo and you feel
vaguely alone, shunned, disdained by your
peers, I would suggest that, for the benefit
of your troubled soul, you knock off a
couple of weeks and travel up to America's
Great Unknown State — Maine. If ever an
alien car had a natural home in the New
World, it is the Saab putting and buzzing
through the black forests of the Pine Tree
State. Once you get inland from the tourist
belt you get the vague impression that every
third car is a Saab, and if it isn't, it's trying
to be.

I've often thought that cars, particularly
the European breeds, have specific geo-
graphical homelands that are clearly defined and in which they are at their best.
England, for example, turns out cars that
seem to be designed specifically to be
worked on in garages on bland milky Sunday afternoons. I've owned several English
marques in my time and have come to the
conclusion that they're not really built to

drive, they're more to *have* and to worry over. The English are by nature putterers. Their houses tend to be fussy, doily-laden, with an aspidistra in every window, and their cars reflect this facet of English character. An Englishman is never happier than when he is spending dreamy endless hours under his Austin A90, a family heirloom, surrounded by spanners and parts manuals.

On the other hand, Italian machines are designed mainly for running down peasantry, scattering chickens, *paisanos* and *Mafiosi* to the winds like confetti, which is also an Italian word, significantly enough — tiny gears screaming, overhead cam motors wailing in defiance. Italian cars, like Italian movie stars, live short, flamboyant, dangerous lives, ruled by the stringent demands of maintaining a public image of *machismo*. No wonder their predominant color is blood red.

The Germans, who appreciate well-oiled efficiency, are at their best creating equipment that has a certain silver grey chromesteel functionality. When they attempt racy, gay frivolity they invariably produce laborious curiosities. A case in point is the Porsche Speedsters, which always reminded me of an overweight Deutsch hausfrau wearing a miniskirt, trying to pass as Sophia Loren. Then of course, there's the Targa. "Targa" is no German word that I know of, so perhaps unconsciously they're hip to the masquerade. Fritz figures if he changes his name to "Luigi" he might make it in the Pasta league.

There has been enough written about American cars reflecting American mores that I won't bore you with a repetition. And like American mores, which today are in a state of total confusion, so is Detroit. But back to the Saab — the toad-like ugliness of this little beast clearly reflects the outlook of a people who spend most of their lives in Winter darkness, up to their behinds in six-month-old snowdrifts, and are somewhat suicidal in nature. A well-to-do middle class Swede thinks nothing of indulging in maniacal head-on games of Chicken on the frozen lakes of his homeland. The Swedes are not a smiling, merry lot. Naturally, the Saab fits the Maine mystique like a glove. The Maine Yankee has never been noted for his spontaneous joy, his *elan,* his animation. To illustrate:

I do a lot of flying in my spare time, and one of my old friends is a superb flight instructor, an ex-crop duster from up in Fort Kent, Maine, about as Maine as you can get. He fits the pattern: silent, tough, sardonic. One day a student was flailing around out in the pattern when Jesse, who was toying with a paper cup of Rat coffee, the kind they always have in airport pilots' rooms, suddenly and without a word got up and ambled out the door. I hollered, "Where are you going, Jesse?" As the door swung shut I caught his twanged answer: "Just thought I'd go out and watch the flames."

Here is a classical example of New England "wit" at its finest, based on somebody else's imminent disaster, laced with a distinct relish for Doom. Jesse Baker, in one sentence, said everything that Ingmar Bergman, the Swedish film-maker, has been trying to say in endless murky breast-beating epics of futility. Jesse once confided to me as we droned along at four thousand feet, practicing Lazy Eights: "It don't pay to take Muskie too serious. He's like all of my Maine relatives. He's got the rest of the country thinking he's smart 'cause he don't say nothing. Maine's been getting away with that for years. They call it Yankee wisdom." He snorted evilly and went back to banging on the Cherokee 180's panel to get the omni working again.

Yankee wisdom is no less a myth than

Swedish sexuality. If you believe that Swedes are sexy you also probably believe that blacks have rhythm, that Frenchmen are unbelievable lovers and that all Italians continually say "Mama mia, dat's a spicy meat-a-ball-a." Oh well. Anyway, the grim, dogged unsexy little Saab is a far more accurate reflection of the Swedish character than any number of Nordic skin flicks, which after all are admittedly part of the dream world. The Saab is real; the Saab is earnest.

I took to escaping to Maine a few years ago when I discovered that within less than four hundred miles of the Triboro Bridge was a state that was literally progressing backward, flaunting all the cherished liberal traditions of twentieth century statisto-mania. That's a nice phrase, by the way, meaning roughly a total hangup on statistics, chiefly those that agree with your already established biases. (Incidentally, I just made it up. If you want to quote it, you'll have to quote me.) But Maine, in the usual tradition of Maine truculence, is simply not going along with the rest of us. While we are having a population explosion they are in the midst of a population *im*plosion. You can drive through dozens of inland Maine towns that give you the spooky feeling of being abandoned movie sets which were used in some ancient remake of *Our Town*. Hamlets with names like Albion, Freedom, Old Testament, China, Ghost Lake, Old Town. Almost all of them have a dark, rushing river that slices right through the main stem. Maine has some of the greatest rivers this side of the Amazon basin, with rolling sensual Indian names: Kennebec, Allagash, Piscatauqua, Penobscot. Next to each one is a tall, gaunt red brick building out of the mid nineteenth century crumbling into ruins, usually with a faded gold leaf sign: DOWN EAST WOOLEN MILLS. You can hear the echoes of Thornton Wilder people under the two-hundred-year-old shade trees.

Personally, I find inland Maine a lot more what I'm looking for than the Coast with its countless "art colonies" and cutie-pie shoppes; its hordes of tweedy ladies who make their own Mexican jewelry and swacky rich kids hanging around Bar Harbor for a couple of weeks before getting back to Choate for the winter. Drive along Route 23 through the Belgrade Lake chain past some of the most beautiful bodies of water in the country; Great Pond, Salmon Lake, Snow Pond, past weatherbeaten mobile homes squatting amid the dark pines. One thing that gets me every time is that almost every Maine farmhouse or shack is surrounded by the hulks of the last six generations of family cars. Apparently the true Yankee never throws anything away; he doesn't even trade it in. He just keeps it in the back yard, in the weeds, slowly sinking deeper and deeper into the subsoil, '63 Galaxies, '56 Bel Airs, '46 Plymouths, '39 Dodge trucks all gradually getting to look like the surrounding rocks; timeless, indestructible, inorganic.

Ralph Nader, obviously a City type who has never *needed* an automobile in order to sustain a semblance of Life, should spend a typical Thursday night on Main

Street in Waterville. Huddled next to the Maine Turnpike, about the only action in town is a guy's car. I drove into Rummel's one night to see what was happening. Rummel's is a place worth driving 200 miles for. Let's face it, if New York is the natural home of majestic pastrami, and it is, then Maine is where ice cream really *happens*. If you're an ice cream cuckoo and haven't dealt with Rummel's licorice, topped off with a ball of Rummel's peanut butter swirl, then you haven't really traveled the ultimate road of ecstasy. I got to talking with this taciturn native who drove an orange-flake GTO, about Life and all the rest of it as we waited in line for our Rummel's double dippers.

"Well, what I do is drive down to Gino's for a while, knock down a cheeseburger, and if nothing's happening I stop off at Mr. Do-Nut. They got this waitress named Barbie who I kid around with for a while. Then I make it over here — Rummel's. I'll probably finish off tonight by making it to Tony's for a Syrian Dagwood. That is, in between draggin' up Main Street four or five times with Ernie in his 427 '69 'Vette hardtop. A real pig."

"Yeah," I answered, trying to sound excited over the full life lived by the swinging youth of inland Maine.

If you get on the Turnpike at Waterville and drive South maybe twenty miles there is a great sign, the only place in the country I've ever seen one like it: MOOSE AREA NEXT 18 MILES. In the Moose Area on either side of the Pike as you drive along you can spot flashes of water through the Norwegian pine and birches and you just know you aren't far from a bull moose that stands seven feet at the shoulders and carries a spread of antlers six feet or so across. I stopped at the Citgo station one night, at the Gardner exit right in the middle of the moose area. I asked the pump jockey: "What about those moose?"

"Yeah," he said, "we see 'em every winter in the cold weather mostly. One day one come out, stood next to that pump over there, shakin' the snow off his back. I like to have wet my pants. He looked mean as hell. One time one of them busts out of the woods back of Gardner and slammed into this VW with a lady in it. Just kept hammerin' at it till he flipped it over. That damn moose musta thought that old VW had come out to the woods to mate with one of them cow moose, and he wasn't havin' none of it. Lemme tell you this,

288

every year or so some guy driving along the Turnpike here hits a moose and it's goodbye Charlie. Hardly ever hurts the moose, but it sure as hell wrecks the Detroit iron. No, buddy, as far as I'm concerned you can have them moose." He went back to chewing on his Harris Deluxe squash doughnut, which is another high-calorie Maine specialty that has padded the hips of many a Maine wench.

When I got back out on the Pike under a brilliant white Northern moon that gets so bright sometimes you can actually read a newspaper by it, booming along through the night, tensed for the charge of a bull moose, it was damned hard to believe that a little over four hundred miles straight south two junkies were probably trying to break into my apartment, deep in the yeasty compost heap of the Village. Ahead of me the inevitable faded maroon Saab with its battered Maine license plate (VACATIONLAND) buzzed like an angry turnip. It was covered with a thick film of cafe-au-lait colored dust, the sort of dust that anybody who has driven in the back roads of Maine lives with and breathes constantly. I hit a patch of mosquitoes suddenly, spotting my windshield like a thin rain of black soot. Occasionally something larger made a juicy "splat" and squirted up and out into the windstream like yellow icing on a birthday cake. Together the two of us, me in my City car, an effete Fiat 124 Sport coupe, he in his dumpy Maine Saab, bored into the blackness through Moose Country.

I flipped on the radio. Up there your All-Transistor Motorola can be used almost as an aircraft ADF. As you boom through the darkness you can tell where you are by what station is getting louder and which one is fading. Portland fades and Augusta grows stronger. Soon Augusta drops down into the birdies and static and Bangor gets stronger and stronger. In between Bangor and Augusta dozens of French Canadians come rolling in; Quebec, New Brunswick, Nova Scotia. Through it all the cool voice of somebody named Ken keeps saying, "Yaz is two for three tonight as he steps into the box in the last half of the eighth. . . ." Yaz is always two for three and stepping into the box late in the game up there in lonely, rolling, beautiful, waterwashed, poverty-stricken Maine.

I finally swing off the Pike at the Waterville-Oakland exit, go past Al's Lobster Pound. There isn't much traffic. There never is by modern standards. I run down the window so I can get a lungful of that sharp, fragrant Maine air. You can just sense big deep lakes all around you in the blackness. It hits me again, that feeling that it's always Fall in Maine. Their summer seems to go by in a couple of weeks, and even in midsummer it feels like fall in the air. No wonder guys like Jesse have a fatalistic bitter humor. In Maine you can almost hear time rushing by while the rocks remain forever. Ahead of me I see the Saab, running high and springy on his home turf, has ducked into a Shell station, probably the second time he's gotten gas in a month. I drive in behind him to top off my tank. In Maine it isn't a good idea to let that needle get down around E, since running out of gas at midnight four miles out of China Lake can be a real bitch. Two rubbery, open-faced little Maine girls wearing hot-pants swarm over the Saab, squirting Super Shell into it and scraping off the bugs. One of them comes back to me.

"What'll you have?" she squeaked, trying to sound like a hardbitten pump jockey.

"Fill 'er up," I clipped, trying to sound like Humphrey Bogart on the bridge of a mine sweeper on the Murmansk Run.

"You know how the gas cap works?" I asked.

"Yeah!" the little round girl hollered from somewhere behind my car. "Guy comes in here with a green Fiat just like yours, only it's green."

Across the street in the gloom I could see Sears Roebuck, a low building not far from Cottle's supermarket where everybody locally stocks up with squash doughnuts and B&M baked beans and diet Moxie. Two more elderly Saabs driven by gimlet-eyed Maine farmers buzz past on their way home from the Baked Bean Supper at the Grange hall in Winslow. Somehow those gutsy little Saabs seem as at home in that country as a beagle rolling in sheep manure. Inland Maine, where the thermometer stands at 30 below most of the winter, with the snow five feet deep and the ice so thick on the lakes that it doesn't break up until late April and then goes out with a roar. It's the way Jesse put it:

"You see, farmin' in Maine ain't really farmin', it's rearranging rocks." He laughed his short mirthless Maine laugh as he said it, and I knew he wasn't kidding.

17

Great Expectations; or
The War of the Worlds
(With thanks to Harold Pinter,
or was it Charles Dickens?)

A ONE ACT MELODRAMA
TO BE PLAYED BY MARIONETTES

Cast of Characters

GROOVY
BUTCH
JOE COCKER

The time is someplace in the fairly near future, damn nearer than you think. At Curtain Rise we see what is by today's standards a totally hip pad. It is crowded with culture symbols of our time: a large inflatable vinyl Campbell Soup can, numerous Peace symbols; doves, clenched fists, a black and white poster depicting rhinos fornicating, Lyndon Johnson playing Clyde while Lady Bird, also holding a machine gun, plays Bonnie, "Make Love Not

War" — a fresco done with Pepsi-Cola bottletops on a background of a tattered American flag drenched with fake mercurochrome blood. The floor is littered with at least 7,000 copies of *Screw, Rat, The East Village Other, The Realist,* et al. A somewhat dusty paper fake Tiffany lamp advertising Heinz's 57 Varieties of Pot dimly illumines the scene.

Naturally, we are deafened by an enormous wave of Acid Rock. Joe Cocker is screaming incoherently *"with a little help from my friends."*

At Curtain Rise the stage is empty. We dimly perceive this between red white and blue flashes of a revolving psychedelic strobe generator, which seems on the verge of blowing a fuse since it hums a lot and occasionally throws sparks onto the burlap-covered floor. We, the audience, observe this scene for thirty seconds or so and then, entering from Stage Right to the sound of an offstage john flushing, we see GROOVY, as he is known among various other pseudonyms. His actual name is Herbert L. Mergenweist, a onetime student in the far distant past at the Bronx High School of Science and several other institutions of doubtful learning. His hair hangs nearly to his waist and seems to be a cross between the Joan Baez Cascade and a ratty Afro. It is streaked with grey. He has a noticeable bald spot. He wears an ancient tie-dyed T-shirt bearing in faded blue letters the legend: WBAI UBER ALLES, worn, hacked-off jeans and an elderly pair of Victor Mature type Roman sandals festooned with bits of corroding chain and brass studs. He is sniffing, and seems to be having a slight nasal problem as his nose runs noticeably. He notices that the stereo is hung up on a groove. COCKER keeps yelling *"wit de help wit de help wit de help wit de help wit de help . . ."*

A look of pained irritation crosses GROOVY's face as though this has happened to him a million times before.

COCKER: (continuing) *"wit de help wit de help wit de help wit de . . ."*

GROOVY speaks, or rather mutters: "Fuck!"

COCKER: (continues) *"wit de help wit de help wit de help . . ."* (He seems to be getting louder and more hysterical, if possible.)

GROOVY rushes across stage, coughing brokenly, and kicks his battered old stereo amplifier, which is on the floor next to a crate of paperbacks. The stereo squawks and COCKER begins to shout: *"friends*

friends friends friends . . ."

Meanwhile, GROOVY has crumpled to the floor, has removed one sandal and is rubbing his foot and weeping silent tears. GROOVY replaces sandal painfully and crawls on all fours across the stage, looking for something. Without warning the stereo begins working again and COCKER goes into the bridge, blaring loudly. GROOVY, scuffling among worn faded copies of *Screw Rat* et al. finally finds what he's been looking for, a book of matches. He sits slumped against his wall at Stage Right, under a large poster of Peter Fonda astride a motorcycle. He searches in his jeans and produces a minute roach which he proceeds to light, eyes shut, inhaling deeply. He sits for a second holding the smoke in, and then suddenly bursts out in a loud, uncontrollable paroxysm of wheezy coughing. His is an air of infinite weariness; dogged tenacity. He sucks again at the roach, sending sparks into the air. Again he coughs loudly.

There is a knock at the door. GROOVY staggers to his feet, grinding the roach out in the palm of his hand and carefully replacing it in the watch pocket of his elderly jeans. Another knock. GROOVY goes to the door, opens it.

GROOVY: (listlessly) "Yeah?"

Enter BUTCH, as he is known to a dwindling few intimates. He is, in actuality, Dwight L. Dingleman. He is somewhat older than GROOVY. He wears a worn-thin pair of narrow-bottomed chinos, an ancient blue basketweave button-down shirt, a thin black knit tie with a large Windsor knot, and decrepit bucks, shoes that have seen many seasons. His hair, what there is of it, is resolutely crew-cut, and he is far beyond mere greying. He wears a madras sport coat, single-button, which is so old you can almost see his shirt through it. He carries a bundle.

GROOVY: "Come on in, Butch." (He speaks casually, comfortably, as though they have done this many times.)

BUTCH: "How's it going, pal?" (GROOVY ignores this, allowing his shoulders to droop in disdain. His whole being exudes put-down.)

BUTCH: "Gee, it's good to see you . . . uh . . . Groovy." (He says the word "Groovy" awkwardly.)

GROOVY: "You're late. I thought I was gonna flip! It was gettin' at me."

BUTCH: "I'm sorry. I know how you feel. I got held up down at Medicare. I was getting jumpy too. It's been three days."

GROOVY: (slumping into inflatable vinyl chair which has been patched many times with rubber cement and vulcanizing patches) "Three days! Shit! It seems like a month. Let's get right at it, before I really blow." (He coughs brokenly and rubs his injured foot.)

BUTCH carefully seats himself on the Campbell Soup can, placing his package beside him.

BUTCH: "Where do you want to begin today?"

GROOVY: (thoughtfully) "Well, we did the Drug Scene number last week. Uh . . ." (He trails off in thought.)

BUTCH: "And the week before that we did the Acid Rock bit. How 'bout Lack Of Communication? We haven't done that in a long time."

GROOVY: (brightening) "Heavy, man! It's been a couple of months. My head's getting together already. Okay. You start."

GROOVY stands up and begins to pace nervously, as though he wishes that BUTCH would leave, radiating truculent impatience. BUTCH watches him for a long moment.

BUTCH: (finally speaking, with great deliberation) "Why don't you get a haircut? For the life of me I can't understand why you let your hair grow like that. You look like a girl! Why, when I was a boy . . ."

GROOVY whirls on him in fury.

GROOVY: "Look, now you see, it's just things like that! . . ." (He lapses into silence after shouting.)

BUTCH watches him, a look of beseeching groping on his face, as though trying to understand yet pained by what he sees.

GROOVY: "All the kids wear their hair like this! It's different than when you were a kid! Everything is different, don't you understand that? The Bomb!"

BUTCH: (quietly) "And those ridiculous clothes. If your mother were ali—"

GROOVY: (rising to crescendo) "That bitch! She never loved me! All she ever wanted to do was watch television all day long, and . . ."

BUTCH: "Don't talk like that about your mother!"

GROOVY: "Hah! Just because she got knocked up and . . ." (He slumps suddenly into his chair, his voice drops back to normal.) "Dammit, Butch, I can't get started today. It's not coming."

BUTCH: "It was starting to work. I could feel that old anger coming back. You wanna start over?"

300

GROOVY: (scratching his stomach disconsolately) "Yeah, might as well. I sure as hell need it. No shit, Butch, I don't know what the hell's happening to the world. They don't have *any* standards. No values. These kids of today don't even think about hair, much less care about it. Jesus Christ! When I was a kid you were nothin' unless you had at least seven pounds of good solid hair. They don't even care any more. I can't get nobody even mad, which shows they really don't care. Wow, when I was a kid . . ." (He trails off moodily, running his fingers through his scraggly greying mane.)

BUTCH: "Why, you *are* a kid. Why, you've hardly turned fifty." (A look of anger crosses GROOVY's face.)

GROOVY: "Look, Butch, how many times have I told you . . ." (His tone is menacing.)

BUTCH: (hastily) "I'm sorry. I forgot. Your generation doesn't recognize years."

GROOVY: "There's only Now, goddammit, only Now! Y'hear that?" (He screams wildly.) "I'm ONE OF THE NOW PEOPLE! I'LL ALWAYS BE ONE OF THE NOW PEOPLE! THERE'S ONLY NOW!"

BUTCH: (nervously loosening his tie) "Now, Groovy, son, don't get excited. I

302

was only trying to help. Maybe we shouldn't do anything today. Maybe . . ."

GROOVY: (crossing over to Butch and patting him on the shoulder) "I'm sorry. I guess we better start easy instead of going right into the Hair thing. That's one thing I just don't understand today. They just don't care about hair."

BUTCH: "*I* still do. You make me mad every time I see you. I want to grab you, give you a shampoo and cut it all off. Make you look like a human being!"

GROOVY: (patting his arm) "That's okay, Butch. It was a nice try. I guess I just don't feel it today."

BUTCH: "Well, how 'bout you starting? Maybe if we work the other way today, like the time you got at me for liking scotch. Boy, that was a great day. I felt good for weeks afterward. How 'bout you starting?"

GROOVY: (shuffling across stage pensively, stroking his beard) "Okay. Lemme think. Uh . . . how's this? . . . uh . . . YOUR WORLD IS DEAD, YOU HEAR ME? DEAD! VIOLENCE AND JOHN WAYNE AND MONEY IS ALL YOUR OLD DEAD WORLD BELIEVED IN! MAKE/LOVE/NOT/WAR!/ MAKE/LOVE/NOT/ WAR!/MAKE/LOVE/ NOT/WAR!" (The last two lines are screamed in a Demonstrator type chant.)

303

GROOVY rushes over to the corner of his room, digs among the rubble for a few seconds and comes up with a sign. It is old and has seen much use. The handle is taped and has been patched up. It is, in fact, ancient. It reads: FASCIST PIG! FREE THE BLACK PANTHERS!

BUTCH rises slowly in anger from his chair, his face reddening.

BUTCH: "Why, you long-haired fag! You pansy! What you need is a good bath. They oughta draft every one of you crummy rotten Hippie bastards. A good First Sergeant would straighten you guys . . ." (GROOVY has now hoisted his sign high and is marching about the room, shouting.)

GROOVY: "FASCIST PIG, FASCIST PIG, OINK OINK, FASCIST PIG, FASCIST PIG, OINK OINK, FASCIST PIG FASCIST PIG, OINK OINK!"

BUTCH: "I'll show you who's a fascist pig, you fag bastard!"

GROOVY: "Fascist pig, fascist pig, oink oink!" (He makes Peace sign with free hand.)

BUTCH: "Beautiful, beautiful! I haven't seen that in years. You're really getting it now, Groovy, you're swinging."

GROOVY: "Oink oink!"

BUTCH: "Turn that goddamn noise down! You call that crap music? Just a lot of banging around. You can't even understand none of them words."

JOE COCKER: (screaming) *"I'll get* HIGH . . . *graaaak . . . I'll get* HIGH . . . *graaak . . . I'll get* HIGH . . . *graak . . . I'll get* HIGH . . . *graaak . . . I'll get* HIGH . . . *graaak . . ."*

GROOVY: "Oh Christ, what a time for that goddamn thing to get hung up. Son of a bitch!" (He throws his sign at the stereo.)

"COCKER: *"Graaaaak . . ."* (stereo now silent)

BUTCH, his face still red with anger, returns to seat; sits down heavily.

BUTCH: "Whew! That was as good a session as we've had in months. That was damn near the real thing."

GROOVY: "Right on! Just like the old days. I'll never forget one day outside the UN, back in the good old days. Jerry Rubin was there. Oh man, what a mind-blower! Dy-na-*mite!"*

BUTCH: (his face lighting up) "Jesus, Jerry Rubin! I ain't heard of him for years. Boy, he used to really piss me off!"

GROOVY: "Yeah, those were the good old days."

BUTCH: "Yeah."

They both sit silently for a moment, contemplating the glorious wonderful past, each lost in his own world.

GROOVY: (somewhat nostalgically) "Hey Butch, you'll never guess what I found today."

BUTCH, still drifting nostalgically in a dream of old wars, merely grunts. He scratches his grey crewcut. GROOVY stands, somewhat arthritically, and peers at his psychedelic light for a long moment.

GROOVY: "You wouldn't believe it. I found a place down in the Village where this little old tailor makes real bell bottoms. Jeez, they're outasight. The kids of today ain't got no style. He says that Paul Krassner comes around once in a while. *He's* getting on, but he's still trippin' out."

BUTCH: "You're right about the kids of today, you know. It's hard to believe it . . . none of these so-called kids hardly ever even *heard* of the Generation Gap. They don't know what they've missed!"

GROOVY: (rifling among the ancient copies of *Screw, Rat, The Realist* on his floor, speaking thoughtfully) "That ain't nothing, Butch. Hardly any of 'em even heard of Wood-stock! And them there has think it's funny. They make fun of it, like those ridiculous marathon dances and stuff."

BUTCH: "Now hold it, Groovy. Don't start knocking marathon dances. Remember, I don't knock Woodstock."

GROOVY: (his long, greying mane drooping disconsolately over his shoulders as he slumps at his table, head in hands) "You know what happened to me the other day? I'm walking down the street, and . . . well . . ." (He trails off, his body racked with sobs.)

BUTCH: "Come on, Groovy. We all go through it. I went through it when your crowd put down Pearl Harbor Day and Okinawa and . . . go ahead, tell me what happened. I went through it, remember?"

GROOVY: "Well, this so-called kid was walking behind me, and he said to another kid 'Hey, there's one of those old Soul diggers!' And then, Butch, they both laughed, and . . ." (He trails off and appears to be fumbling for a match in his jeans. He finds it and tries to light what's left of his roach. He coughs violently.)

GROOVY: (gasping) "I can't . . . smoke as much grass as I used to. Gets me in the throat." (Hack Hack)

BUTCH: "Yeah, I know. I can only have one finger of scotch a day, and I'm really not supposed to have that."

307

GROOVY: "And then, Butch, you know what he said?"

BUTCH: "No! Don't tell me."

GROOVY: "Yeah. He said, 'He's one of those old Love Generation freaks. Boy, the one thing I'm never gonna do is get old. Man, I can't stand old people.' " (GROOVY ends this sentence with a sob, lowers his head to the table. BUTCH pats him on the shoulder.)

BUTCH: "Don't worry, Groovy. You get used to it."

GROOVY: (sobbing) "But I'm a Youth! My generation invented Youth! We *are* Youth! Who the hell are these phonies? My generation invented Youth. They don't *listen* any more."

BUTCH: "Yeah, I know. My generation invented Guilt. And who cares any more? Jesus, those were the days. God, I can remember when every editorial, every record, every play, every book, every cartoon did nothing but tell you how rotten guilty you were. God, it was great! You don't know how good it feels to have everybody tell you that *you*, personally, ruined the world. Man, that's power!" (BUTCH is excited at this point, obviously exulting in and savoring his guilty past.) "God, I remember one day when five SDS activists tied me up in my swivel chair and took turns hitting me with rubber hoses, all the while hollering 'Make Love, Not War.' One kid knocked the cap off this back tooth." (He points to tooth) "And another grabbed my ear with a pliers and . . . God, it was great!"

GROOVY: "Stop! I can't stand it! Those were the days. These idiots today never heard of Warhol, or . . ." (He trails off.)

BUTCH: "Yeah, but you never heard of Billie Holiday, or even Miles Davis."

GROOVY: "Now look, Butch, don't get sore. Remember, we're in it together. We can't start fighting now. We're about the only survivors left of the old Generation Gap war. We can't start hassling."

BUTCH: "Yeah. We need each other. You can't have no Communication Gap without me. And how the hell can I have any guilt without you?"

GROOVY: "Yep. You old bastard. You never could understand Soul."

BUTCH: "Horse shit. You never could understand *swinging*."

(There is a pregnant pause at this point, and then Groovy, staring straight out at the audience, speaks in a low voice.)

GROOVY: "Yeah, but *they* don't understand either one. We only got each other, Butch."

BUTCH: "What the hell *do* they understand?" (He suddenly brightens as if he has remembered something.) "Hey Groovy, wait till you see what I got. It cost me an arm and a leg and then some, but . . ."

GROOVY: (laughing sardonically) "Holy Christ, an arm and a leg and then some. I haven't heard that expression since my Old Man left the scene. Arm and a leg. Wow, man, you talk like an old Pat Boone movie."

BUTCH: (ignoring him) "I came across it in Brooklyn, in this shop a little old lady runs. I couldn't believe it!" (He carefully unwraps his package on the table, obviously afraid of breaking what is inside.) "Look, there it is. How do you like that? A genuine, mint condition Little Orphan Annie Ovaltine shake-up mug!"

GROOVY: "Yeah, I guess it's all right if that's where your head is at. Wait'll I show you what I just got. This'll really blow some charges with you. A real skull buster!" (He rushes over to orange crate and scrabbles amid the paperbacks, with a great flourish whips out an object.)

GROOVY: (announcing triumphantly) "A genuine, working, absolutely authentic

Spiro Agnew watch!"

BUTCH: "My god, I'd almost forgotten. The Silent Majority! Let's use that in our next session. We haven't even touched on the Silent Majority. I forgot all about it!"

GROOVY: (getting excited) "Yeah, I'll dig out my old IMPEACH NIXON buttons, and I got one that shows Agnew with a Pig face, and . . ."

BUTCH: "This is gonna be great! I'll bring my hard hat."

GROOVY: "You got a real hard hat?"

BUTCH: "Yep. It's yellow. It's got an American flag on it."

GROOVY: (excitedly) "Oh, wow. Zap! And I'll dig out my Viet Cong flag, and we'll . . ."

BUTCH: (his voice tense with anticipation) "I got a bumper sticker that says: AMERICA. LOVE IT OR LEAVE IT. And I'll . . ."

GROOVY: "Don't tell me! Surprise me. I can hardly wait. It'll be like the good old days again. When people really hated with style, and life had *meaning!*"

BUTCH: "And you can hit me with a rotten egg, and I'll . . ."

GROOVY: "Don't spoil it! Let's wait till the next session. Outasight, man, it's starting to happen already!"

BUTCH: "You're right, Groovy. Say, does that Agnew watch say ten minutes after *ten?* Already? My doctor says I have to get to bed by ten o'clock every night, and . . ."

GROOVY: "Yeah, I can't stay up as late as I used to either, what with my sinus headaches and . . ."

BUTCH rises, carrying his shake-up mug, dodders to the door and pauses before the threshold.

BUTCH: "Groovy, can I play my Harry James records at the next session?"

GROOVY: "Great, man! That'll really bug me."

BUTCH opens door and departs. We hear him from offstage.

BUTCH: "See you next week, same time, and if you really get jumpy give me a call and we'll fight over the phone."

GROOVY: "Hang it all out, babe. I feel together again."

BUTCH leaves. Rock booms out. GROOVY squats on floor, a lonely aging figure, fumbling for a match. He lights his roach and coughs a wheezy, rasping phlegmy hack as

THE CURTAIN FALLS

18

Little America,
I Love You

Some things I know . . . I just know.
Driving along those highways and
throughways and those state roads all
of my life. Never knew a real home.
Motel, motel . . . Howard Johnson,
Holiday Inn and Eddie's German Cottages. One day I know, I just know, I'll
drive up a long hard road to that great
Holiday Inn In The Sky and that mean
old neon sign will be winkin', blinkin'
NO VACANCY, NO VACANCY . . . Move
on.
— anonymous 20th century driver

God knows how many motels have swal-
lowed up nights of my life, from Florida to
Maine, from Pennsylvania to Oregon, down
to Juarez. My god, what motels, what highways. Sometimes I think there are a few of
us who love highways and motels more
than the places they go to or the momentary stopovers they are. The other night I'm

sitting in the bar at Downey's, a saloon on 8th Avenue, a couple of hundred feet west of Broadway in mid-town, gazing around at the old photographs on the walls of actors peering out of dressing rooms, wearing make-up of long forgotten characters. Marilyn Monroe kissing Eli Wallach, Geraldine Page looking tense. Somehow they all seemed on the road, at least at that moment, since I was on my second Tanqueray martini. The guy I was with, a shoddy slippery Producer of borderline pornographic off-Broadway "artistic triumphs" was in a vaguely maudlin mood. The maudlin is not to be confused with true sentiment, certainly not in the vicinity of the Lunt Fontaine, anyway.

SHODDY PRODUCER: (touch of sob in the voice) "Sometimes I wonder what it's all about. Guy does his best and in the end you don't come up with nothin'. Look at poor Marilyn there. Jesus!"

ME: "Yeah, you're right, Jay. Sometimes you wonder what it's all about." (This last said with great solemnity, as though intoning a newly discovered Universal Truth.)

SHODDY PRODUCER: "You know, ever since *Princess Lesbia Meets Su-*

perman closed in New Haven I've been feeling rotten. I gotta get out on the road again. I don't feel right unless I'm in some hotel room dialing Room Service."

ME: "I know how you feel. Some guys are Hotel guys, and then there's Us."

SHODDY PRODUCER: "Us? What do you mean?"

ME: (signalling for a third martini) "Motel men. We ain't the same, Jay, deep down. You ain't living unless you're in a hotel, and me, hotels make me nervous. It's Motels I love. Man, some nights when you're booming along out there under the stars and you see that Howard Johnson coming up out of the blackness, well . . ."

SHODDY PRODUCER: "Motels? You mean those tourist cabins?"

ME: "Tourist cabins? Where the hell you been living for the past hundred years? You mean you don't know what Truman Capote said about motels?"

SHODDY PRODUCER: "Truman Capote? Wasn't he the guy who wrote *Grass Harp*? A bomb. The B'nai Brith hated it. What the hell does *he* know?"

ME: (my voice assuming a low philosophical narrative tone) "Jay, let me tell you about motels. Bartender, bring my slippery friend here another Tia Maria, or

315

whatever the hell that slop is he's drinking, and I will tell you something about motels."

SHODDY PRODUCER: "It's getting late, and . . ."

ME: (interrupting) "I have listened to you for many a night, telling me of the disasters of your life. Allow me a few precious moments of your time. And anyway, I'm buying."

SHODDY PRODUCER: "Okay. I got nothin' to lose, I guess."

ME: "How truly spoken. We, all of us, come into this world with nothing and we leave it in the same state. Hairless at the beginning; hairless at the end. A great cycle of futility that stretches . . ."

SHODDY PRODUCER: "I thought you were gonna tell me something about Motels."

ME: (carefully twisting lemon into gin) "Motels, ah yes, they are part of it. There is nothing more American than a motel. I have traveled the world over and I find few places anywhere on this globe remotely like a good motel, and I for one love them. Motels, Jay, are like green oases on the trackless desert, snug ports nestled on the shores of endless alien seas."

SHODDY PRODUCER: "No kidding?"

ME: "No kidding. No, I kid you not, as Captain Queeg often said. Some nights when I'm cooped up in my pad on 10th Street I feel the urge to revisit some of those great motels I have seen in my time. You know, there's nothing that makes you feel as free, as on-the-move, as a motel and there's nothing I like better than being free and on-the-move."

SHODDY PRODUCER: "You can't tell me nothin' about being on the road. Did I tell you about the time I was traveling with the third road company of *Pajama Tops*? We was stayin' in this tank town outside of . . ."

ME: (raising my hand imperiously) "Hold! Avaunt, as the Bard so nicely put it. I have the floor. Have you ever heard of the name 'Camino Real'?"

SHODDY PRODUCER: "Are you kidding? Maureen Stapleton. For Chrissake, what kind of a dumb ox do you think I am? Have I heard of 'Camino Real.' Tennessee Williams. Why, I remember the night the . . ."

ME: "I mean the *real* Camino Real. Not some wispy melodrama about ladies with roses in their teeth. The real Camino Real."

SHODDY PRODUCER: "You mean

there's another one? I wonder if the rights are still . . ."

ME: "Jay, some day I think you're going to try to buy the rights to the world, including serial, recording and book club sales. The Camino Real, the *real* Camino Real, is a magnificent motel that once enfolded me with its loving arms like a passionate mistress on the dark desert sands."

S.P.: "Holy Christ! No kidding?"

ME: "Yes, Jay, the Camino Real is a fantastic motel across the bridge from El Paso, just outside that decadent, exciting fleshpot of the Western world — Juarez. You come up on it all of a sudden, like some movie set rising out of the red and yellow baked clay. It's made of adobe, and has high, swinging balconies and long cool open-air hallways with cactus, and you can smell the chili beans and hear some guy playing the guitar someplace down by the pool.

"And what a pool, with that Mexican sun slanting down, making the water dance and shimmer until it looks like cool liquid blue ice. And the girls just lay stretched out like lizards in the sun. The rooms have low ceilings with that square, heavy Spanish furniture made out of some kind of hard, dark wood and I lay flat out on that big bed the first night I signed in, picking up Mexican music from some tinpot radio station, with all those cornets and bugles and maracas.

"Why, Jay, they've got a nightclub in that motel that looks like it's right out of a set of some old Merle Oberon movie, with all these elegant ladies in slinky gowns and these guys dressed up in black, formal suits going up winding staircases, with chandeliers made out of cut crystal and a band wearing those Mexican shirts with the puffy sleeves and their hair slicked down like patent leather. Out in the lobby they

have a little cart that they push around, ladling out free ice-cold lemonade, with that hot desert air puffing in once in a while to remind you that there are mountains somewhere around."

SHODDY PRODUCER: "Aw, come on, you're not talking about a *motel*."

ME: "The hell I'm not! You have known me as a car cuckoo for a long time, Jay. Well, any good car nut is also a motel nut. Cars and motels go together. In fact, they are almost one and the same. I figure it couldn't have been more than 20 minutes after the first car ever built set off across country than some smart guy figured that the guy driving it would have to eventually look for some place to light, empty his bladder and rest his weary head, so he put up a sign on the side of a shack reading: HONEYMOON ACRES TOURIST CABIN and that's where it started. I've been in motels all over the country, all kinds, and sometimes me and other Motel cuckoos get together and swap stories about great motels we have known.

"I remember one outside of Jacksonville, Florida, just over the Georgia line, made out of old faded warped wood with blistered paint. A couple of kitchen chairs in the room; linoleum on the floor, and a light bulb hanging down from the ceiling. There was an old geezer on a rocking chair sitting out in front of the office, which was about half the size of a Manhattan phone booth, swatting flies and chewing tobacco. I drove in my drophead Morgan Plus 4, hot and tired after making 700 miles that day heading South toward the Keys. Cost me six dollars that night, and as I lay on that mattress, which felt like it was filled with corn shucks, I could hear the crickets and those Florida frogs quackin' outside in the warm dark. I went out around the side and got me a Coke out of the machine, came back and lay in the dark drinking Coke and listening to frogs and Tammy Wynette singing D-I-V-O-R-C-E on the radio, and I want to tell you, that night I knew I was in the South as much as I'd ever be, and I could hear those big diesel rigs rumbling on past, carrying those oranges up North. Now, I don't think of that motel much, but when I do I can just smell that blistered paint and hear those crickets chirpin' away."

SHODDY PRODUCER: "Stop, you're making me cry! It's like that speech in *Orpheus Descending* about them night birds that are born without feet and they keep flying around . . ."

ME: "Horsefeathers, Jay. I ain't talking about Tennessee Williams country, I'm talking about the *real* South. Where US 41 goes snaking down through the swamps all the way from Chicago through Georgia, past all those beautiful motels with their NO VACANCY signs and . . ."

SHODDY PRODUCER: "US 41? Never heard of it. Is that over by the Lincoln Tunnel, in Jersey?"

ME: "US 41 in Jersey! My god, you really are an innocent. You mean you don't know the feel and smell and look of the really great roads of America? Forty-one! Just saying it makes shivers go up my spine. US 30. US 66. US 80. You name 'em, Jay, I been over 'em all. The great Turnpikes: Maine, Florida, Indiana, Ohio. They're like the great rivers of the world — the Nile, the Amazon."

SHODDY PRODUCER: (stirring his drink listlessly) "Jeez, I never would have known. Where's US 80?"

ME: "Ah, I hoped you'd ask. On US 80, my Showbiz scoundrel, lies one of the greatest motels of them all. Have you ever heard of Little America?"

SHODDY PRODUCER: "Yeah. Isn't that that place where that Admiral Byrd or whatever his name was had all those penguins and polar bears? I saw a documentary once on NB. . . ."

ME: "No, Jay. One of the great moments of my driving life, which has been most of my life and I wish I had a dollar for every mile I've driven, came one bad day on US 80. I was heading East out of Salt Lake City in a rented Cougar. She was in good shape, with a set of good rubber, and I crossed the Wyoming line about seven o'clock at night. It was in October and all day the sun had been hard and bright and crystal sharp, and you could see for a million miles to the low hills that lay on either side of US 80, which is a fast divided four-lane masterpiece that runs as straight as a die East and West along the lower part of Wyoming, my absolute favorite state. I was trying to make Cheyenne when all of a sudden, with no warning at all, it started to snow, that wind cutting 90 degrees out of the North, right across the highway.

The snow was coming down so fast and hard that I felt I was driving through a white tunnel and I couldn't see fifteen feet ahead of the Cougar. Right ahead of me I could barely make out the red taillights of a big semi, and I figured I'd hang on to him like grim death, since I figured he could see the road. It got colder and colder, and my windshield was freezing up faster than the defrosters could blow it off.

I had the radio turned to a station in Rawlins, Wyoming, and they began giving out emergency storm alerts. Let me tell you, you've never been in a blizzard until you've been in a real Wyoming screamer. Well, I figured all I could do was push on. The night was so black that nothing existed except my headlights and all that snow, and those two faint taillights up ahead. Well, I hung on to the back of that semi like a barnacle, and I could see another guy hanging on to me off in the haze through my rearview mirror. We boomed on through the night. It seemed like forever. Then, all of a sudden I saw a sign, barely visible through the snow off to my right where some range cattle were huddled up in a snowbank next to a barbed wire fence. LITTLE AMERICA FIVE MILES AHEAD FREE ICE CREAM CONES.

The sign was shaped like a penguin. For a second or two I thought, Christ, my mind has snapped, at last, I know this snow is bad enough, but 'Little America'! But no, it was really there. The wind howled and the snow kept getting worse and worse. Temperature must have been down around zero when I came to this turn-off with a big arrow: LITTLE AMERICA.

Well, I pulled off, swung under the underpass amid the snowbanks, and the next thing I knew I was driving into the biggest goddamn gas station I ever saw in my life. They must have had two hundred pumps, and there, spread out before me, was one of the greatest motels of them all. Little America. I went into the lobby, and I can't tell you how good that heat felt after that night on US 80.

I think I must have got damn near the last room, and here I was in the middle of nowhere, at Little America, on the edge of the void, in a room that had crystal chandeliers, Florentine furniture, silver candelabra, blood-red velvet walls with a carpet so thick I sunk up to my ankles. Outside the wind howled and the antelope came nuzzling up to the glass windows of my room. I wandered down to the dining room where they had fresh Rocky Mountain trout and baked abalone, and one of the greatest bars in all creation, where everyone sat around drinking Jim Beam and laughing at the storm that raged outside.

Why, Jay, Little America is the only motel in the world that has its own Post

Office. It's a whole town. This storm kept up for three days. They kept reporting hunters lost in the hills. And every night I'd come back from that fine Wyoming food and that good Wyoming liquor; lounge around under my crystal chandelier, with my candelabra gleaming and the red velvet walls glowing like blood, and I figured that if there's anything finer than a motel named Little America in a storm, I sure as hell don't know about it."

SHODDY PRODUCER: "Hey, that gives me an idea. Have you ever thought of writing about a motel? See, there's this poor waitress, kind of a Kim Stanley type, see, and this guy comes in off the road on a cold night, and he's on the lam, see, and . . ."

ME: "Oh for Chrissake, that's *Bus Stop*."

SHODDY PRODUCER: "A bus stop ain't the same as a motel."

ME: "That reminds me, have I ever told you about the Inn of the Six G Flags, outside of Fort Worth? Now there's a place that . . ."

19

Abercrombie's Bitch

NOTE: The following transcript has been edited somewhat for inclusion in this psychiatric journal, mainly for reasons of space. It represents the key session in the analysis of a patient whom I shall call Abercrombie. His disturbance has as yet not been cataloged in the literature of Psychiatry. I herewith submit the evidence, and have tentatively called this Complex, for working purposes, Abercrombie's Bitch.
— Dr. Abraham Strauss

The patient, a Caucasian male aged thirty-nine, had appeared in my offices voluntarily and without reference eight months prior to the transcribed session. He claimed he had found my name "in the Yellow Book," which did not seem significant to me at the time. Most of our sessions were held in the late afternoon, and he usually appeared at them in a somewhat agitated state, occasionally defensive and evasive. He maintained that his sex life was adequate and satisfying; his relationship with his off-spring Mark, 9, and Herman, 13, was in all ways normal, with only the usual amount of bickering. His wife, Marcia, 31, Caucasian, was unaware of his visits. The following transcript took place at 3:30 p.m. April 5, 1972, in my office.

ABERCROMBIE: (after lying stretched out on the couch for some three minutes in silence) "Where'd you get that clock?"

DR. STRAUSS: (caught off guard) "Uh . . . what was that?"

ABERCROMBIE: "Hmmm." (lapsing into silence) (At this point he began plucking nervously at the naugahyde up-holstery of my Barcalounger.)

DR. STRAUSS: "Look, Abercrombie, have you ever thought that maybe there's nothing really wrong with you, that you like a little nap maybe every afternoon?" (I was using the Abell Schnauzer Cross-grain Technique in an attempt to "get at" Aber-crombie. I had attempted this before, but with little success. Today it was different. c.f. *Abell Schnauzer, "Notes: Vienna,"* Vol. III, pp. 123–26) "Look, Abercrombie, I've got patients with real problems, and . . ."

ABERCROMBIE: "You know, you can get one of these with a vibrator, like a buzzer or something, built in, and it jiggles your back."

DR. STRAUSS: "Get what?"

ABERCROMBIE: "One of these Barcaloungers. I've got one that tilts, and it jiggles me. And it's got a portable bar built in the arm. You just tilt it back and . . ."

DR. STRAUSS: "Look here, Abercrombie, let's cut out the small talk. I can't sit around every afternoon and . . ."

ABERCROMBIE: (his voice rising in excitement) (I noticed his pupils were somewhat dilated.) "I also got one that has a hammock attachment that you can swing between trees, and . . ." (His voice broke at this point and he began sobbing uncontrollably, a clear example of convulsive diaphragmatic emotional nerve charge related to secondary traumic self-revelation. I leaned forward, sensing a breakthrough.)

DR. STRAUSS: "There, there."

ABERCROMBIE: "Oh God, I can't stop. Please help me, please! I can't stop. Oh, Doctor . . ."

DR. STRAUSS: "Stop what? Just tell me about it, Abercrombie. Just relax and talk."

ABERCROMBIE: (in a low voice, his fingers plucking at the Barcalounger) "I'm so ashamed, doctor. It's getting so that I can hardly face my family. Some nights I think it's all going to come out, and I can hardly drag myself home." (He pauses, head buried in hands.)

DR. STRAUSS: "Yes. Go on. What are you afraid will come out? You can trust me, old man."

ABERCROMBIE: (taking deep breath, dabbing at his eyes with a Kleenex) "Doctor, I just bought a Remote Control Transistorized Rotary Home Barbecue." (I waited for him to go on. We sat for a few moments in silence.)

ABERCROMBIE: (in a hoarse whisper) "Now you know." (pause; a deep breath as though gathering strength) "Yesterday I bought a set of stainless steel matched Corncob Pipe Making Tools, in a leather carrying case."

DR. STRAUSS: "I didn't know you smoked."

ABERCROMBIE: "That's just it! I don't! But I couldn't help myself!" (I was beginning to realize that Abercrombie was no ordinary patient. A new, highly developed Complex was slowly emerging.)

DR. STRAUSS: "Abercrombie, I want you to close your eyes and just talk."

ABERCROMBIE: "Sometimes I think Marcia suspects, and God, what if the kids found out! I knew that I had to do something about it a few months back, when I was playing with my new electrically operated Sure-Catch-Em Bait Casting Reel. It was raining out. I could hear the rain banging on the roof, and I don't know, it just got me that day. I looked around at all of it, and I knew I was damn near at the end of the line, and . . ."

DR. STRAUSS: *"An automatic electrically operated bait casting reel?"*

ABERCROMBIE: (brightening) "Yeah, it's great. It has a cross-hair sight on it. It hooks on to any type of spinning rod. You just hit the trigger with your thumb and zappo, it shoots your lure out maybe a half a mile if you want. It uses these mercury batteries, and . . ."

DR. STRAUSS: "Fishing is a relaxing hobby, and I'm glad."

ABERCROMBIE: "Oh, I don't go fishing or anything like that. I just like this reel. I got a bobber that lights up when a fish bites, and I like to turn that off and on, too."

DR. STRAUSS: "You were speaking of the rain on the roof, it seems to me."

ABERCROMBIE: "Oh yeah. Well, you know, doctor, I was just sitting there and I got to thinking that I needed help of some kind, after I went for that amphibious

331

ATV with the . . ."

DR. STRAUSS: "ATV?"

ABERCROMBIE: "All Terrain Vehicle. With a folding duck blind that has these plastic reeds and cattails." (At this point I suspected the patient was hallucinating. However, subsequent investigation has proved that there *is* such a device, and his description was accurate.)

ABERCROMBIE: "It cost me damn near four grand, and I was already up to my ass in debt, what with the three snowmobiles."

DR. STRAUSS: "*Three* snowmobiles?"

ABERCROMBIE: "Yeah, not counting the one that I traded in on the Honda Scrambler. Jesus! I knew I had to do something after that ATV, you bet. They always say that you can live with the soft stuff, but when you start hitting the hard ones you better watch it."

DR. STRAUSS: "They? Soft stuff?"

ABERCROMBIE: "I'm not the only one, you know. We can tell each other. I know a lot of them. You see them at lunch hour, and Saturday mornings at Sears, and . . ."

DR. STRAUSS: "See whom?"

ABERCROMBIE: "Us! There's this one guy who hangs around the Tool department who's really gone. This guy has a thing on socket wrenches. He must have twelve million dollars' worth of socket wrenches stashed around."

DR. STRAUSS: "Socket wrenches? Is he a machinist?"

ABERCROMBIE: "Hell, no. He's a TN. Got a thing on socket wrenches. Jesus, they're the worst. He don't use 'em, he just buys 'em."

DR. STRAUSS: "A TN?"

ABERCROMBIE: "Yeah, Christ, they're the worst. Them TNs got a mean streak in 'em."

DR. STRAUSS: "Excuse me, just what is a TN?"

ABERCROMBIE: "Oh Christ, I forgot. You're not one of us. A TN is a Tool Nut. That's just what we call 'em in the trade. They're mostly harmless."

DR. STRAUSS: "The trade?"

ABERCROMBIE: "Yeah. I started as an RB. A guy over in Bloomfield Heights turned me on." (At this point Abercrombie was relaxed and seemed to be almost enjoying his confession. At the time I was as yet unaware of the implications of what he was saying.)

ABERCROMBIE: (continuing) "God, I'll never forget it. I was just wandering around on my lunch hour, looking in store windows along Sixth Avenue when this guy standing next to me looking in this window said, 'Boy, those Japanese jobs are something! There's one that picks up the Weather band *and* Sonar as well as FM.' At first I didn't pay any attention to him, but then I noticed he was panting, and was sweating a lot. I said, 'Sonar?' He answers, 'Yeah, it makes a kind of buzz. You never know when you might need it to navigate with.' Well, to make a long story short, I bought this thirty-nine band Japanese radio that got Sonar and I noticed the other guy bought one too, and everybody in the store seemed to know him. It was the beginning. I still see him around, and he's gone down hill a lot and looks kind of seedy, the way RBs get in the end."

DR. STRAUSS: "RB? Does that refer to . . . ?"

ABERCROMBIE: "Yeah, you guessed it. Radio Bug. A lot of us get started on soft stuff like radios and work up. 'Course, Radio Bugs like to pretend that it's just a harmless habit, no worse than maybe martinis, but don't you believe it."

DR. STRAUSS: "Yes? What happened after you bought the radio?"

ABERCROMBIE: "Well, the next day I

see another one in a window over on 42nd Street that had a special band that got the Mexican ball scores. Which mine didn't. So I picked it up. And then a couple of days later I spotted this stereo FM tuner that was built into a Viennese beer keg. You turn the spigot on and the sound comes out of the bung hole. So naturally I figured it would go good in the den, and since Marcia's birthday was coming up I wasn't really being extravagant or anything. I figured I could kill two birds with one stone. I should have known then what was happening. Especially after she got kind of sore when I turned the beer keg on and it blew the fuses in the basement, and one of the kids got a shock from the bung hole. After I got the matched Wrist Radios and the Walkie-Talkies, things began to change."

DR. STRAUSS: "In what way?"

ABERCROMBIE: "Well, I got in with this gang of ACs who hung around Hammacher Schlemmer on a lunch hour. I started with a Radar Instant Hot Dog Frizzer. The radio thing was getting a little touchy around home, and we had a lot of fun with the Frizzer the first day."

DR. STRAUSS: "Frizzing hot dogs?"

ABERCROMBIE: "The only trouble is,

we're both on diets all the time, so we don't eat hot dogs. We just frizz 'em. It's got a Radar Proximity Radiation Indicator that lights up when the hot dog is frizzed. You ought to see it go. The kids love it."

DR. STRAUSS: "But if you don't eat hot dogs, it seems to me . . ."

ABERCROMBIE: "Yeah, there's that, but it is great to see it light up. It's got this buzzer that goes off. And then I brought home this Handi Insta Cuberino. She really blew her stack on that one."

DR. STRAUSS: "Handy Insta-Cubereeno?"

ABERCROMBIE: "Damnedest thing! Makes ice cubes in twelve and a half seconds flat, in any shape you want. It's got these little plastic molds. You make ice cubes in the shape of footballs, turtles, and they got this naked girl one for parties. You put this coloring stuff in, and you can make red, white and blue ice cubes in twelve and a half seconds."

DR. STRAUSS: "I see."

ABERCROMBIE: "I got two of them. In case one blew out during a party. You never know. Then, the very next day, at Macy's, I come across this Musical Ironing Board that had a tape deck that played Rock so that Marcia could kinda groove when she was doing the ironing. Only trouble is, one of the rubber feet fell off a couple of days after it came, and the dog ate it. So we stuck it in the basement. Among with the Electro-Pop that I got her for Christmas."

DR. STRAUSS: "Electro-Pop?"

ABERCROMBIE: "Pops corn. It's transistorized. There's something about anything that's transistorized that gets me right down in the gut. Just the word is kinda nice to say: *Transistorized!* Gives you a feeling of security. You know, Doc, like it's Now. Yeah, it pops corn. You just set it and it squirts this low-cal butter on the popcorn when it's done. We only used it twice, because of the hum. Made Marcia's teeth hurt, so she stuck the Groove-A-Rock Ironing Board down in the basement next to the Electro-Pop, and that's when she found the thirty-seven transistor radios that I hid under the basement stairs."

DR. STRAUSS: *"Thirty-seven?"* (It was here that I suspected that he was showing a typical Slanski Numero Exaggerative Syncope; *ALD Journal, Proceedings, December 1935, entry 762, [incl.] Isadore Slanski.*)

ABERCROMBIE: "Yeah, I was getting

337

embarrassed about them. And I began to have trouble finding places around the house where I could hide stuff."

DR. STRAUSS: "Excuse me, Abercrombie, but what is a . . . how did you put it . . . AC?"

ABERCROMBIE: "Ha! I keep forgetting. You're not one of us. An Appliance Cuckoo, of course. I know one guy bought twenty-three turnip dicers in one month alone. Talk about a monkey!"

DR. STRAUSS: "Appliance Cuckoo, hmmmm."

ABERCROMBIE: "It gets you gradually, and the next thing you know you're on the street." (He slumped despondently; his voice lowered perceptively. He was going deeper into himself.) "One day you find that all you can think about is the next thing you're going to buy. You can't think of anything else! I remember one time: I'm making love to Marcia, and I kept thinking of that two-cylinder convertible lawnmower, with a trailer attachment where you can carry beer bottles when you're mowing the lawn, and I could tell she knew something's wrong. You know, I can't sleep sometimes, knowing what drove me to the top at the agency. Everyone . . ." (Patient sobbed briefly and went on brokenly.) "thinks that I'm dedicated. Ha, what a joke! Boy, that's a hot one. Dedicated to my work! Doctor, I *gotta* make dough! I'm a Vice President because I got this goddamn monkey on my back. Doc, do you know what it costs to spend your lunch hours at Abercrombie & Fitch? And your Saturdays at Sears, and Wednesday night at Montgomery Ward, and all the time reading catalogs and sneaking down to the Post Office with your coat collar rolled up so nobody will recognize you to pick up your stainless steel Swedish wind-up apple corer from Haverhill's? I gotta bust it, I gotta do something! Oh my God, where'll it ever end?" (Abercrombie began to pace furiously. He stopped suddenly, and his whole mood changed.) "Hey Doc, where'd you get that great looking Lucite clock?"

DR. STRAUSS: "My wife picked it up somewhere. I never notice those things."

ABERCROMBIE: "You never notice those things! My God, that's *all* I notice! And you haven't heard the worst. I got a monkey on my back that weighs in at better than five hundred dollars a week. There hasn't been a week in two years that I haven't spent five bills! That Marcia never knows about. She thinks I'm knocking down twenty-five thou at the agency, when last year I was good for fifty-one, and I'm up to my ass in pawn checks!"

DR. STRAUSS: "You say you're a . . . an . . . AC?" (I wanted him to expand on the term for my own professional reasons. Somewhat unethical, I'll admit, but in the interest of Science. I perceived that Abercrombie's case could well be seminal.)

ABERCROMBIE: "I was. Then I moved into the big stuff. Like my Aqua-Skoot. That started it." (He trailed off.)

DR. STRAUSS: (after pause) "Yes? Go on."

ABERCROMBIE: "That god damned Aqua-Skoot! Me and Howie from the office were on the seventh floor of Abercrombie & Fitch when he spots this damn thing, and I knew I hadda have it. It was all I could think about for three whole days, and I finally went in and popped for it."

DR. STRAUSS: "You say an . . . Aqua-Skoot?"

ABERCROMBIE: "Yeah, they're these motor-driven water skis. Twelve hundred bananas! I got so scared of what Marcia'd say after I bought 'em that I hid 'em in the mail room at the office. And then I got this Cine Slica-Drive, which is this indoor driving range that shows movies of famous

340

fairways, like in Honolulu, and you hit this goddamn golfball, and you pretend like you're playing against Arnold Palmer, and his score is flashed up on the screen. Christ, Doc, I don't even play golf! Thirty four hundred smackers! Thirty four hundred! The goddamn thing weighed a ton. How the hell could I have them deliver *that* at home? I knew that the guy in the mail room would flip, and I hadda do something!"

DR. STRAUSS: "There, there." (He was getting hysterical and I was afraid he might slip into a typical post gravital decline. Drs. Emory, Knabell, *Yokohama Psychiatric Quarterly*, Volume III, pp. 9 and 10 ibid.)

ABERCROMBIE: "You don't know how it is. It's hell! It was even worse than when I was going through the HWM scene. God, it took me six months to break that one. Even now, sometimes I find myself going back on it!"

DR. STRAUSS: "HWM? Is that some sort of drug?"

ABERCROMBIE: "Christ, I wish it was! That would be easy to handle. Doc, an HWM is one of the worst kind. A Home Workshop Maniac! You can blow your whole goddamn life on it. Jesus, do you realize you can get a home Blast-O-Forge that's a whole home-operated foundry, where you can mold sinks and make Christ-knows-what!? Fenders for your car! Steel pogo sticks! They give you plans for all of them. Oh God almighty, where will it end? It goes for seventeen thousand, not including jackhammers! You get the HW thing going and you're damn near a gonner. I know one guy has a home workshop worth damn near fifty thousand big ones. And all he ever made on it was a Chinese ormulu knickknack table. He don't give a damn about making things. He just likes to go down and pat the machines. He just moved into a bigger house so he can put a drop-forge out in the garage in case he wants to make his own nails. He figures if you make your own nails you can save dough, since the drop forge only costs twelve G's! But that's the way the HWs think, and I was one of the worst, do you hear that, I'm admitting it! But I still can't stop!" (At this point Abercrombie lapsed into silence. I felt it best to allow him to continue at his own pace, utilizing, of course, the technique so brilliantly developed by Dr. Stefan Schnauzer in his work with the Albertson Psychiatric Advisory Unit. His, Abercrombie's, silence

342

was timed on my chronograph at four minutes, seventeen and three-tenths seconds.)

ABERCROMBIE: "Doctor, it's getting late and I don't know how to tell you this. You won't think I'm sick or anything, will you? But last summer I took the *final* step. I fought it. God knows how I fought it! But there was no way out. After the Slica-Drive I knew I had to do something. This thing came in a box car! Now don't get me wrong — it's beautiful. I'd do it again, I tell you! I love to just turn it on and watch those fairways pop up and down, those lights flash on and off, and Jack Nicklaus' score or Sam Snead's rings the bell. But I hadda do something, see? I had stuff hidden in the trunk of the car, in the garage, in my office, I even had nineteen lockers at Grand Central Station that I had to stick quarters in every day."

DR. STRAUSS: "Yes, Abercrombie, what did you do?"

ABERCROMBIE: "I rented a warehouse in Brooklyn!"

DR. STRAUSS: (Admittedly I committed a gross breach of good technique, but I was startled and failed to conceal it.) "A warehouse? Really?"

ABERCROMBIE: "Almost a block square. Three stories high. I'm looking around for another one. I'm running short on space. Every night, after work, I go and sit and look at all my great things. Sometimes I run a can opener, or hook up my magical Race-O-Track and run the cars, or maybe I just go and plug in some radios, but those hours that I spend in my warehouse are the only times that I know peace, Doc. But deep down inside, I know it's not right, and I just gotta get this monkey off my back."

DR. STRAUSS: "Sorry, Abercrombie, your fifty minutes are up. Shall we continue next Tuesday?"

ABERCROMBIE: "I don't know, Doc, if I can afford it. I just ordered this Fold-A-Slope, and I don't know if I can continue with you."

DR. STRAUSS: "Fold-A-Slope?"

ABERCROMBIE: "Yeah, it's really great! I saw it at Abercrombie & Fitch last week. It's a folding ski slope. See, it's got this big electric motor, and the snow goes upward and you stand on it on your skis. And there's this fiberboard screen that shows pictures of the Canadian Rockies, and . . ."

DR. STRAUSS: "Excuse me, Abercrombie, but my next patient is waiting."

ABERCROMBIE: "Not only that, but it

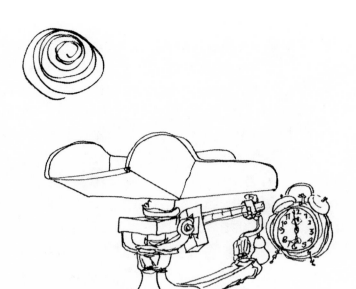

has this polyethylene snow that is wash-
able, and you can do shusses, and if you
turn up the speed they've got this Giant
Slalom attachment where you can go
around these rubber barrels, and . . ." (At
this point I rang for my nurse, who over-
powered Abercrombie who appeared to be
going into a fit much like the one reported
by Dr. Emil Orbach in his provocative
essay *Ein Kleine Nachtmusic; A Problem,
Proceedings of DLO, January, 1913.*
Using the standard armlock she quickly
had him out in the street.)

Prognosis: Abercrombie is suffering from a
comparatively new, yet widespread malady

which seems to have primarily affected males of the Western Hemisphere: compulsive and insatiable hunger for useless yet highly symbolic gadgets, coupled with a well-developed sense of guilt and associated manic defense mechanism. I am conducting further experiments on this Complex, which bears the tentative appellation Abercrombie's Bitch.

Dr. Abraham Strauss
New York, 1972

20

Lillian

The other day I came plodding through the rubble on Sixth Avenue, a colorful sordid concrete gash that splits the underbelly of Manhattan like the Yangtze River carves up China, wading through beer cans, cigar butts and split-open bags of garbage to the corner of 14th Street. Ah, Sixth and 14th, the crossroads of Hades, where vice meets chicanery, where avarice meets greed, where George Plimpton and Gloria Steinem never tread. The light for me was red and the big neon sign flickered DON'T WALK. Being basically part of that now tiny minority who believes that when the sign says DON'T WALK, you don't, I clumped to a halt. I love to walk in Manhattan. I have never once been bored, although I'll admit I have felt many other emotions. At times stark fear has gripped my vitals; at others total amazement at yet another bizarre revelation. Occasionally complete mystification at some passing enigma, but never — I repeat never — boredom.

The watery Manhattan sun filtering down through layer upon layer of drifting effluvia imported from New Jersey, the Garden State, casts an oddly artificial Broadway Stage lighting over the scene. Real natives, and I am one of them in this town, take advantage of that phenomenon by costuming themselves and using odd, bizarre makeup that goes well with the vast surreal stage that is Fun City. Anyway, I'm standing there on the curb next to a short, stout creature of aggressively indeterminate sex clad entirely in black leather cut to a medieval pattern — complete with gauntlets, breastplate and coat of arms — when a monster Cummins cab-over-engine diesel tractor roared up to the corner and stopped for the light. It towered like some fearful beautiful engine of war over the scurrying throng; its chrome gleamed balefully; the vast expanse of windshield glistened with a green light like the eye of Cyclops. It was a hell of a machine. I could feel 14th Street quiver under the rolling beat of its idling lethal diesel power plant, a kind of taut, deep-bellied thrumming. Across its cowl, in flowing romantic script, was the name *CYNTHIA*.

The driver, his elbow casually draped out the window, was puffing away on a yellowed, burnt-out Missouri meerschaum. He wore a fake Miami Dolphins blue, orange and white football jersey. He fitted the cab of that Cummins the way Joe Namath's hand fits a football. They belonged together. A faint silver-grey cloud of Prince Albert smoke drifted out of the cab to join the noisy 14th Street air. I couldn't help it. There was something about the way he lounged in that cab; the way that big mean tractor squatted there. I had to make contact. I hollered up at him amid the din:

"THAT'S A HELL OF A TRACTOR YOU GOT THERE!"

He peered down from King Kong's forehead and gave me a long, squinting hard look. I guess I passed.

"THANKS, BUDDY," he yelled over the muttering diesel.

"HOW COME CYNTHIA?" I hollered back.

"THAT'S 'ER NAME, STUPID," he answered with perfect logic.

"A HELL OF A GREAT-LOOKING TRUCK," I shouted while my fellow Manhattanites, including the bird in the leather armour, looked at me as though I had sprouted poison oak leaves from my nostrils and had a fin running down my back.

"YEAH," he answered, "SHE IS GREAT. BUT SHE CAN SURE BE A BITCH WHEN SHE WANTS TO."

The light changed and Cynthia bellowed with a thunder that drowned out even the IRT below our feet and roared off in the direction of Cheyenne or Albuquerque. Automatically my feet began to move in the distinctive Manhattan shuffle, which takes years for a newcomer to learn. It is a kind of single-minded porcine waddle, head thrust forward and pulled down deep into the shoulder blades, knees bent, body at a distinct forward angle to better ward off unexpected buffets or crippling blows. The gait is most closely approximated by that used by the male warthog on a cross-country grub rooting expedition. I swung into the Chock Full O'Nuts for my afternoon chocolate brownie and while I waited, perched on those tiny ass-punishing stools which are deliberately designed to drive you off of them in pain after a maximum of sixteen minutes in order to keep the traffic moving and the cash register ringing, I thought back on Cynthia and her partner the Corncob Kid. Yep, I thought, I'll bet Cynthia can be a hell of a bitch at times, but then *every* Cynthia can be touch and go. The girl slapped my brownie down in front of me with a surly flip of her wrist.

"Coffee," I barked, "black." She curled her lip in disgust in the classic Manhattan manner.

"Here y'are." She banged the cup down in front of me with an adept, practiced wrist movement which neatly slopped the scalding coffee over my thumb and into the guts of my very nervous wristwatch.

"That'll be fifteen cents more," she muttered with the remote, infinitely-bored non-contact voice of the human automaton who sees nothing, hears nothing and gives out even less. She waited while I fished out the change and then left to harass another customer. I sipped the Chock Full O'Nuts coffee, which in spite of everything is still great, and thought on about Cynthia — which naturally led me to another machine I had known: Lillian.

By God, Lillian, I thought. Jesus, I haven't thought about her for years! Every guy who has ever spent a good part of his life behind a steering wheel knows that after man and machine have spent enough time together, in good weather and foul, over pothole and rutted gravel, each begins to soak up some of the character of the other until finally the man is forever

changed, however subtly, by his association
with that particular machine and the machine, like a worn shoe, has bent and
molded its way of being to fit his. Any time
you buy a used car you can sense a
stranger riding with you, complaining,
hawking and spitting and smoking things
you wouldn't touch in a thousand years. I
don't know who got to Lillian before I
came across her, but she must have had a
hell of a life.

It was during a bad stretch I was going

352

through. School was getting boring. No money. And I had a bad case of the Total Itch. So I scratched around and picked Lillian off a used car lot in South Chicago. A '51 Hudson Hornet that looked like somebody's kid brother had repainted it on a Saturday afternoon using Woolworth Black Gloss Enamel, the kind that goes on in little lumps, and a brush to match which distributed its hairs along with the paint. It was cheap, which was more important than the crummy paint.

Every week I began booming up the length of Indiana, up U.S. 41 to see a girl I had a thing on. Looking back on it, I can't see why since she was even meaner than Lillian and her paint job wasn't so good either. I put maybe five hundred miles on Lillian every weekend, two hundred and fifty up and two hundred and fifty back, not counting all the screwing around to the drive-ins and stuff in between.

At first Lillian was a total stranger, like all alien used cars are. I'd find strange hairpins and sinister bottlecaps under the seats. The last guy who'd had her was some kind of a wine freak or something because she always smelled of that 69¢ a quart Mexican tokay that guys who own Hudson Hornets tend to drink. Sometimes

353

on those long hauls I'd get to wondering what he was doing and whether one day we'd have to fight it out in some parking lot if he caught me and Lillian, the way guys fight over girls that they don't care for any more.

All that summer me and Lillian hauled ass up to Chicago and then back, through heat and rain, through lightning and June bugs. We had plenty of close calls, like one time south of Indianapolis at four in the morning some damn farmer cut right out of a cornfield, out of a gravel road with an unlighted Chevy pickup and I to this day don't know how the hell I missed him. At 90, in a Hudson Hornet, things happen fast. All I remember is a scared white dumb face going by me so fast it was blurred, with the Hornet leaning over on two wheels and my Allstate baldies screaming. We had a couple of others that summer which left their mark too, like the one outside of West Lafayette when the tractor-trailer up ahead in the rain suddenly jack-knifed and me and Lillian slid sideways for what seemed like two miles and finally came to rest a couple of feet from that damn truck with our front wheels in a culvert.

As Fall came on and it started getting

colder Lillian began to change. By now I was pouring enough oil in her to fuel a GMC diesel, and forget the gas. It was on a cold late Fall night, with a little snow in the air, at about three in the morning that I began to notice a new sound. Me and Lillian had come so close together now that I knew every fugitive squeak and every piston slap with total intimacy, the way you get to know a girl's voice after you've lived with her so long you don't even have to hear it any more, you just *know* it.

Way down deep in her guts, somewhere below the floorboards, her transmission began muttering, just muttering at first, a kind of under-the-breath bitching the way old men do sitting in all-night bus stations, just growling now and then. All the while old Lillian is banging along, laying down her characteristic cloud of blue-black smoke on 41. We went along maybe forty more miles and I began to notice the growling was picking up; the muttering was more distinct and delicate-like, I turned down the Philco radio that had a little Hudson triangle trademark on the middle of the dial to listen to that mean growl. I bent my head over a little to get my ear nearer the floorboards. Like every other machine I've ever known, as soon as

I listened for the growl it stopped.

Well, I figured, I'll let her think I don't notice it. This is always a good strategy, but it doesn't always work. We proceeded on into the night with our usual total clattering, smoke-breathing harmony. Then she started up again. I hummed to myself to throw her off balance, to make her think I wasn't listening and turned up my ears. Sure enough, the growling picked up. It was then that I recognized what Lillian was saying, over and over that beatup Hudson transmission was distinctly saying, with a rasping, growling voice: *god damn you god damn you god damn you god damn you* just over and over and again. There was no doubt about it. That's what that bitch was saying: *god damn you god damn you god damn you god damn you.* . . .

That night something changed between us. For the first time I saw that babe in Chicago for what she was. We had a dingdong fight in a bar on the North Side that ended with her yelling: "GOD DAMN YOU, I DON'T NEVER WANT TO SEE YOU AGAIN!"

I paid the check and went out and got in Lillian, her smelling of that crummy tokay as usual, I headed her south, and then she started up: *god damn you god damn you god damn you god damn you* . . . over and over. For the full two hundred and fifty miles.

I got rid of her the next week. Sold her to a guy in Rushville, Indiana. Lillian is probably still roaring around somewhere, swearing at whoever owns her. I never missed her and I know she never missed me. No doubt because she really belonged, in her heart, to that guy who guzzled the tokay and had the girls who left hairpins under the front seat.

21

The Ferrari in the Bedroom

Slowly and mechanically, without really seeing anything, I leafed through the pages of a big fat silky ladymag. My mind was barely ticking over, receiving no inputs, producing no output. (Have you noticed these days that minds don't have ideas; they have *concepts;* they don't have stimuli; they have *outputs.* Jesus, if we work hard enough and fool with the language enough we may be able to *will* ourselves into becoming foolproof transistorized computers capable of beating those IBM monsters at their own game.)

I leafed on, one small corner of my inner being carrying on its continual battle with the imps of hell which keep raging down there, begging me to get started on my true career as a firebomb terrorist or a graffiti-scrawler. Now I'm not the kind who spends much time looking over gurley-mags of the *Cosmo* stripe, although I find their banner headlines on the cover page more than slightly great:

FORTY-NINE NEW EXCITING ORGASMS, A Smashing Color Feature!

Or:

FIFTY-THREE FAMOUS WOMEN REVEAL THEIR TOP SECRETS FOR SENSUALITY!

Sensuality, I thought listlessly, that's the new big *Cosmo* word. Last year the big word was "Fun." The year before it was "wild." Everything was "wild." Too bad they don't have good old sexy women any more. Sensuality is in; sexy is out. Or, a real chiller, from the same issue, blunt and to the point:

WHAT TO DO WHEN HE WON'T MARRY YOU

Holy Gloria Steinem, I breathed, hurrying faster through the steaming pages filled with quivering, Jello-y gurley-prose. I skimmed through *WHAT YOU CAN LEARN FROM FRENCH GIRLS*, which was a hell of a letdown since it yammered on about how to dress, when actually the best thing anyone can learn from French girls is how to *un*dress with style. *THE COMPLETE GUIDE TO ENCOUNTER GROUPS* held me for a second or two. Complete Guide, I thought, what the hell is a Complete Guide? Some of the best encounter groups I've ever known in my life happened like spontaneous combustion in the back seat of a Pontiac, and you sure as hell won't find them listed in the Complete Guide. Oh well.

My mind takes these evil turns when I'm squatting nervously in my dentist's waiting room, which is where I infrequently have my torrid encounters with the world of Rona Jaffe and Helen Gurley Brown. The dog-eared *National Geographic*s had long since palled and I find *The Orthodontist Quarterly* curiously unrefreshing. In the next room, the arena, I heard muffled moans and occasional subdued thumpings. Some other poor devil was on the rack and it soon would be my turn. My dentist is an odd duck, as most of them are. He paints water colors and smiles enigmatically as he scans the X rays. A man who has peered into the gaping maws of caries-ridden humanity has few illusions. The thin whistling whirr of the highspeed drill mingled with the soft tones of Muzak as I tried to concentrate on *FORTY-NINE NEW EXCITING ORGASMS.* I flipped another page.

Without warning it got me full between the eyes — ZONK!

VARROOOOMMM! New excitement in the bedroom! The now look in groovy exciting varooomm-y beddy-time Fun! Made of high-impact top grade vinyl, this authentic copy of a real racing Ferrari will add the excitement and speed of Monte Carlo, Sebring and Le Mans to your nocturnal hours. Available in Italian Racing Red, British Racing Green and Chaparral White. At better stores everywhere.

The quivering copy undulated across a spectacular four-color double-page spread. It showed a bedroom displaying obvious signs of being inhabited by someone exceedingly well-heeled and spectacularly hedonistic. The decor was conventional, standard Department Store Mod except for that varoom-y exception. There in this haven of rest, in the spot where the bed used to be in the good old days, was what looked like, at first glance, a brilliant blood-red Ferrari roadster.

Mama Mia! I muttered as I so often do these days after being forever influenced by an Alka-Seltzer commercial. I convulsively crossed myself, which is somewhat surprising since I am not Catholic, but since I've seen plenty of ballplayers and wrestlers do it on the boob tube I figure what the hell, you can't lose anything by trying. *Mama Mia,* a Ferrari in the bedroom!

For a crazy instant I thought, what a great title for a Sophia Loren pizza-opera co-starring Marcello Mastroiani as the aging world-weary Italian architect who one day meets this girl on the train for Sorrento and . . . Cut it out! That gets you nowhere.

I examined the ad closely. Sure enough, there it was. It was not a vagrant hallucination. A bed shaped almost exactly like a Ferrari. It even had vinyl wheels with vinyl knockoff hubs; STP and CASTROL decals plastered all over it. I instantly knew what I was seeing. (I have this way of instantly knowing these things.) I was looking at a true masterwork of Slob Art, fully worthy to stand beside the concrete Mexicans, the Seven Dwarf lawn sprinklers and the Praying Hands day-glo reading lamp in the pantheon of true Slob Art.

I was interrupted by a sudden ringing shout of pain from the next room as my fellow victim became forcibly aware that he had a nervous system and it was sensitive as hell.

Jesus! We've got this thing about making stuff to look like other things. Second-rate restaurants disguised as derbies; radios disguised as Brunswick three-hole bowling balls, ball-point pens sneakily passing as cigars. Some psychologist could do a hell of a paper on this subtle undercurrent in American life. But — the Ferrari in the bedroom: Now *dat'sa* spicy meat-a-ball-a!

Immediately my monster intelligence, which was influenced in infancy by William Inge and Smoky Stover, conjured up a scene. The dentist's waiting room with its forty-nine new exciting orgasms and its limp water colors faded and I found myself magically peering into an analyst's inner sanctum of the Future:

A distraught citizen lies writhing on the couch. The analyst of the future, his hair hanging in great waves to the floor, wearing blue isinglass shades, squats like Buddha behind his mother-of-pearl desk.

The dialogue begins:

ANALYST: (hereafter referred to as
A) "Come, come, Witherspoon,
you've been here every day at three
for seven years and I, for one, am
getting damn tired of it."
DISTRAUGHT PATIENT: (hereafter
referred to as DP) "I know, Doctor,
but . . . but . . . but . . ." (He hurls
himself to the floor where he lies
kicking off his shoes in a muffled
tantrum.)
A: "Look, Witherspoon, I know it is
unprofessional of me to tell you to
get on the stick, but for God sakes,
man, if I can use the expression, I
didn't spend fifteen years in training
to listen to you snivel and whine.
There must be some reason why you
have a blind, insensate, totally de-
structive hate and fear of all Italian
cars."
DP: "I know, Doctor, but . . ." (rising
to his feet, his eyes hollow, staring.)
A: "No buts. Let's can the crap.
What's bugging you, Jack?" (It is obvious that A is a practicing representative of the emerging school of
Guts Psychiatry which has recently

364

discovered that a kick in the ass is worth ten thousand logged hours on the soft down of the couch.)

DP: "All right, dammit! I've got to get it out sometime!" (He screams incoherently, beating his fists on the wall.)

A: "Watch it, Witherspoon." (A squirts DP with a plastic fire-extinguisher.) "You've been seeing too many Jules Feiffer movies, Jack. Now cool it."

DP: (his voice low, tremulous, breast heaving) "All right. I'll tell you what's eating at my very soul."

A: "It's about time, Witherspoon. You can't go around forever chopping up Fiats and Maseratis on the streets with a fire axe and escape the booby hatch."

DP: "I know, I know! I try to control myself, but just the sight of one of those red devils with all them STP stickers all over 'em drives me out of my mind. Everything goes black and I . . . I . . ."

A: "You don't have to tell me what you do. I had to bail you out three times last month alone. And those guys from Allstate Insurance are starting to get nasty."

DP: "Doc, do you remember Clara?"

A: (caught off guard) "Clara? What's she got to do with Maseratis?"

DP: "Plenty!"

A: (affably lighting up a joint) "Aha! So, just as I thought. I knew sex was behind it somewhere. Go on. Spill it."

DP: "You remember me telling you about how much I loved her, how from the first time I saw her that afternoon in the rain at the Orange Julius stand eating a brownie, that I had to have her? You remember me telling you about that? Do you?"

A: "Of course. I have it in my notes. You never did tell me how that all came out."

DP: (stifling a sob) "That's just it, Doctor. I haven't been able to face it till now. Clara is the only girl I've ever loved. Her eyes! Her skin! The way she smiled in that mysterious way, like the girl in the Unscented Arid commercial on TV. My God, she's a goddess, a real goddess! I plotted night and day to get near her, to caress her, to fondle her, to whisper sweet nothings into her alabaster ear, to lay my life down for her, . . . to . . ." (He breaks off, choked with emotion.)

A: "There, there, Witherspoon. Here, have a drag on my joint."

DP: (unhearing, lost in his own world) "Six months went by and then it finally happened. All my dreams were about to come true. I had wined her and dined her, taken her to every rotten musical for miles around, and then, one night with the moon shining in her eyes I asked her to come up to my pad. She had never been there before. I was afraid to ask her. She said in that beautiful deep voice, like Candy Bergen's: 'Why, yes, Virgil.' "

A: (leaning forward, savoring the story) "That must have made you feel good, eh, Witherspoon? What happened then?"

DP: "I bought wine, flowers; burned incense. Got the pre-amp on my stereo fixed. And then, that night after dinner — which I had prepared from my *Julia Child TV Cookbook* — I swept her off her feet in the candle-light and carried her into my bedroom. I could feel her lithe pulsing body underneath the shim-

367

mering gossamer she wore that night."

A: "Yes, yes. Go on, man!"

DP: "I slipped out of my H.I.S. bells. I saw a brief flash of alabaster flesh in the faint shimmering moonlight, and then, and then everything blew up in my face. All that I had hoped for, dreamed for exploded before me."

A: (breathing heavily in excitement) "What happened?"

DP: "She laughed. . . . *Laughed!!* My God, it was terrible. Have you ever had a girl laugh at you in your own bedroom? It was terrible. At first I couldn't believe my ears. That insane laughter in the dark. I asked her 'What's wrong? Why are you laughing?' and then . . . then . . . she said it!" (His voice trails off in sobs.)

A: "Said *what?*"

DP: "She said, 'What the hell's that cockamamie thing?' I answered, 'It's my Varrooommmm Ferrari Bed. It adds new zest and exhilaration to beddy-by time.' And . . . *she* said, 'A plastic Ferrari? With pillows? And STP stickers? Jeez! I seen some nutty scenes in my time . . . I been with plenty of kooky johns that go for bullwhips and track shoes. But lemme out of here! I don't want nothin' to do with any plastic kiddy-cars. What kinda freak do you think I am?' And then, Doctor, she hit me in the mouth with my Yogi Bear FM radio and ran out. I never saw her again. And ever since that night I have this uncontrollable urge, every time I see an Italian car, to . . ."

A: "That's enough, Witherspoon. I've heard enough! I've listened to sick stories in my time myself, and you're damn lucky I don't have you tied up right here and carted off. Don't bother to come back. We don't need your sort around here."

DP: "I understand, Doctor. Please forgive me."

A: "Get out of here, you bum! If there's anything I can't stand it's your kind of Sickies. And anyway, your 55 minutes are up." (The scene ends with DP skulking out into the night, carrying an axe, hunting for a helpless Fiat 850 fastback.)

For a long moment I sat watching in the fetid, chewing-gum-laden theater of my mind the scurrying departure of DP as A took a final drag on his roach and prepared to greet his next patient.

"You're next. And how's that little old wisdom tooth this week?"

"Varroommm!" I blurted out involuntarily.

"What was that?" My dentist, a hardened customer thickly calloused by the tartar of Life, eyed me narrowly.

"Uh . . . bruummmf! I was just clearing my throat."

"I thought you said 'Varroom.' "

"Why no, Doctor, that's silly. Why would I say varoom?"

"Search me, pal. Now, let's get down to that wisdom tooth." I bravely marched into the torture chamber, ready to take the worst he could give me.

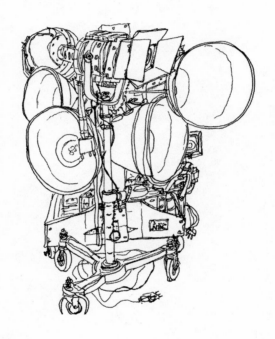

About the Author

For many years a cult radio and cabaret personality in New York City, Jean Shepherd was the creator of the popular film *A Christmas Story*, which is based on his books *In God We Trust, All Others Pay Cash* and *Wanda Hickey's Night of Golden Memories* and has become a holiday tradition on the Turner Network. He was also the author of *A Fistful of Fig Newtons*. He passed away in 1999.

The employees of Thorndike Press hope you have enjoyed this Large Print book. All our Thorndike and Wheeler Large Print titles are designed for easy reading, and all our books are made to last. Other Thorndike Press Large Print books are available at your library, through selected bookstores, or directly from us.

For information about titles, please call:

(800) 223-1244

or visit our Web site at:

www.gale.com/thorndike
www.gale.com/wheeler

To share your comments, please write:

Publisher
Thorndike Press
295 Kennedy Memorial Drive
Waterville, ME   04901